Japanese Memories

By Ethel Howard

DEDICATED TO THE MEMORY OF MY BELOVED HUSBAND

The Past is gone, yet echoes still remain: Sweet memories of love, sad memories of pain. Then let us learn of each, and, day by day, Strive to retain the good and throw the dross away The Truth will live, we only need the Real To guide us onward to the Great Ideal.

H. A. B.

AN ACKNOWLEDGMENT

I should like to take this opportunity of expressing my grateful thanks to Lady MacDonald for her generous help and encouragement during my work in Japan, and also for her great kindness in allowing me to use the photographs, taken by the late Sir Claude MacDonald, which add so enormously to the value of my little book.

E. B.

FOREWORD

THE contents of this book are primarily personal experiences of a seven years' stay in the house of a Japanese nobleman, having been gleaned from jottings in my diary and such reminiscences as my memory recalls. In writing of a country so steeped in centuryold traditions and of a people so loath, in many ways, to adopt Western culture, it is necessary to introduce a little history at the outset, for the reader will have to familiarize himself with certain strange names and systems that had dominated the social order in Japan without change for generations, and still influenced both ruler and ruled at the time of my arrival in that country in 1901.

Since the house of a Daimyo was my destination, it will be perhaps well for me first to explain the meaning of that title, and the standing and identity of such an all-powerful nobleman as the Prince of Satsuma. Up to 1868 Japan had a Feudal System, and under the Emperor there was a Viceroy or Military Suzerain, known officially by the title of "Shogun," who swore fealty to the Emperor, and in his turn had as his vassals the Daimyos or dukes of the country, who were some two hundred and sixty-seven in number. The Provinces of Japan were formerly governed by Daimyos under the Shogun, to whom they paid homage, and their vassals were in turn the Knights of their own Province, who as a class bore the name of Samurai.

The Samurai of old had very high standards of duty loyalty and obedience to their lord and master being foremost. Their sword was the very expression of their soul, a weapon for defending right and subduing wrong. They regarded all kinds of trade as beneath them, never coveting gold, and, in fact, preferring poverty as being decidedly more honourable than riches. In their eyes it would have been an insult to receive payment for any duty rendered to their lord. But they expected of their Daimyo that his soul should be that of an ideal warrior, of a brave fighter untouched by the things of this world, and for this reason he was kept as a recluse in his castle.

The Shogun was appointed by the Emperor, who was given a free choice in the matter until 1603, when Iyeyasu was appointed to this office. He was a member of the Tokugawa family and a man of tremendous influence, and for two hundred and sixty-five years from his being appointed the Shogunate remained exclusively in the Tokugawa family as an hereditary office. The appointment was still nominally made by the Emperor, but he was compelled to offer it to a member of this family.

As time went on the Shogun became more and more powerful, and the Emperor ceased to take any active part in the affairs of government. He resided in Kyoto, the capital, and lived in complete seclusion, the Shogun visiting him once a year to pay homage as his vassal. The Daimyos lived half the year in their own Province and during the other half in Tokio, by command of the Shogun, who resided there, and who fixed the time for their yearly visit. When the day came for a Daimyo to visit Tokio it was a very big undertaking. He was carried in a palanquin, with curtains all round it, and was accompanied by a large retinue consisting of a number of pedestrians and a few horsemen.

There is a long, lonely road leading from Kyoto to Tokio called the Tokaido road, along which the Daimyos' processions used to pass. At the present day many pilgrims are to be seen walking along it in white kimonos and large broad-brimmed hats, each carrying a red blanket and a piece of matting by way of a bed. There is also up at Nikko a most beautiful avenue, with rows of fine cryptomeria trees, which were planted as a memorial by the Daimyos after the death of Iyeyasu. No words can describe the beauty of these trees, with their dark foliage and deep shade, through which fairy gleams of light play between the branches.

When the Daimyos passed along the roads the route was cleared and no human being was permitted to show himself. These feudal lords were considered too great for mortal eyes to behold, and if by chance anyone met a Daimyo's procession, it was expected that he would immediately conceal himself behind the trees or bushes on pain of a prompt order of " Off with his head! " In every house along the road the doors and windows had all to be closed. The wives of the Daimyos resided mostly in Tokio, by the Shogun's orders, being kept there more or less as hostages.

Gradually the rule of the Shogun became quite unbearable. He had taken complete control of the Government, and never consulted the Emperor; he had collected an enormous military circle round him in Tokio, and by various large payments had induced merchants and men of all professions and crafts to settle there. His influence appears to have spread to the Samurai, who also by degrees got entire control over the Daimyos, since the latter, living in complete seclusion, took scarcely any exercise and were rarely seen or spoken to. Consequently they became physically and mentally weakened, until they were quite unfit to rule and unable to think or act for themselves. In spite of the power the Samurai exercised they still did obeisance to their lord, and always prostrated themselves in his presence. But they forced him to say and do all they demanded, and held his purse so tightly that he did not even know the extent of his wealth and possessions. They gave gifts in his name without his knowledge, except when the time came for him to be thanked. They built and enlarged his houses, and managed his affairs so completely that he himself became in the course of time merely a figure-head. As the Japanese idea of true dignity and greatness is a stoical endurance of pain and sorrow with no outward show of feelings, the Daimyo's face had under all circumstances to be entirely expressionless.

It is with the Province of Satsuma, in the South, that my reminiscences are chiefly concerned. This was one of the most important of the Provinces, whose Daimyo is said to have been formerly the richest and most powerful of all the barons; the ratio of his vassals among the population having been calculated at twentyfive per cent, as against five per cent, of the other Provinces. The inhabitants of Satsuma are fighting men of a typical seafaring kind, exceptionally strong in physique, who may be compared with an English type such as Charles Kingsley graphically described in " Westward Ho! " and other novels. " Rough diamonds " in plenty are to be found among them, besides an endless array of brilliant leaders and commanders in both Services. Among the soldiers I may mention the great Commander-in-Chief, Oyama, Nozu, Kiroki, etc.; and among naval men, the famous Togo (the Nelson of Japan), and countless well-known Admirals and Commanders. There is, in fact, an old saying among the men of Satsuma that if Japan were valued at one hundred pounds their Province would have to be estimated at half that price. So that, historically speaking, the Province is exceptionally interesting one of its most notable personalities having been the Daimyo Tokahiro Shimadzu, ancestor of Prince Tadashige and his brothers.

It was in Kagoshima, the capital of Satsuma, that the first service held by missionaries in Japan took place in the sixteenth century. But the Jesuits who had settled in the country, and more particularly in the South, became so powerful that the men of Satsuma began to resent their influence; and in consequence the door was gradually closed to all foreigners, Japan isolated herself, and for many years no Englishman could enter Satsuma, so prejudiced had the clan become against outside interference.

Long afterwards, however, the men of Satsuma encountered the English under very painful circumstances.

In 1863 Japan was in a ferment of unrest. The tyranny of the Shogun was becoming unendurable, and the clans of Satsuma and Choshu (an adjacent Province) conceived the notion of getting rid of the Shogun and investing the Emperor with full authority. This was reported to the Shogun and his adherents, and a large gathering of Daimyos was convened to take counsel on this matter.

At the height of the excitement the Duke of Satsuma's procession was passing along the road that led to Tokio, when a party of English people, including a missionary, Mr. Richardson, unwittingly crossed the path of the Daimyo and his retainers. They knew nothing of the ancient law by which the people were expected to clear the way and to conceal themselves. The Daimyo' s escort regarded the presence of the English as an insult to their lord, and drew their swords, with the result that Mr. Richardson was murdered.

The Foreign Powers naturally resented this unfortunate encounter, and a big indemnity of 25,000 was demanded by the British Government from the Duke of Satsuma. The Daimyo at first refused to pay this sum, and ships were sent to bombard his capital. The Satsuma clan soon realized their inferiority in modern warfare and sued for peace, but in consequence of this incident a very sore feeling against foreigners rankled for several years. After prolonged negotiations a Treaty was signed between the Shogun and the Foreign Powers. No permission, however, had been obtained for this by the Shogun from the Emperor or the country, and in consequence great wrath was excited, particularly among the Daimyos. The clans of Satsuma, Choshu, and subsequently two others, rose against the Shogun, determined to displace him by force, and to give the Emperor full powers. The Shogun at this point tendered his resignation from a sense of duty, and his office was relinquished for ever.

In the following year the Daimyo of Satsuma gave up his fiefs, and the other Daimyos soon followed his example. Finally, in 1871, the clans were all abolished, and the late Emperor became absolute in authority. He recognized that it was essential that Japan should no longer isolate herself from foreigners, and that she must become equipped on equal terms for social intercourse, trade, and competition in the markets of the world. From this time the country began to develop.

The Emperor's residence was moved from Kyoto to Tokio, where the Shogun's castle was converted into his palace, and the city itself became the permanent capital of Japan in place of Kyoto, which had been the capital for one thousand years.

Notwithstanding the abolition of the old feudal laws, the spirit of the former system took long to break, and it was in pursuance of the new policy that the appointment was made which placed me in charge of Prince Shimadzu and his young brothers. This appointment was the more remarkable from the fact that in the whole of Japan no house had openly acknowledged the friendly relations with England by introducing a foreigner as a resident into their home, until the House of Shimadzu one of the greatest among the nobility entrusted me with the care of the young Princes, and placed their education in my hands.

Their grandfather had been created Prince. He was a famous hero, who did much for his country, especially in regard to its naval develop ment. The father of Prince Tadashige (my eldest pupil) had died in Kyoshi when his son was only twelve years old, and the boy lived for a time in his own Province, among his retainers, entirely according to the ancient regime, as one who was too great to converse face to face with any of his people an attendant being always at his side.

Being thus left an orphan, and brought up in the Shinto creed of ancestor worship, the tenets of which are essentially connected with the religion of the Imperial family, this young Prince was called upon to bear heavy responsibilities, both in serving the spirits of his ancestors and in attaining such a standard of noble life as the Satsuma clan set before him. He early learned to recognize that he must live up to his great name, and that hundreds of retainers looked to him not only as their master but as a wise example. When he took his father's title he had to make a public vow before them all. Later on I was permitted in confidence to read the contents of this vow, and very beautiful it was but terribly solemn. Such words are too sacred for publication, but well might this young Prince present the grave and earnest appearance which was so noticeable to me on my first presentation.

Fortunately, he was exceptionally gifted, both physically and mentally, and was too young for the enforced seclusion and inactivity to have affected him. But he was guarded as a priceless treasure, and had not been allowed, up to the age of eleven years, even to ride alone in a jinricksha, having always used a double one with his attendant sitting by his side for protection. Two years after his father's death, however, he was taken to Tokio and placed as a daily scholar at the Nobles' School. Shortly after this a still greater change was made, as I was appointed to the care of the Prince and his brothers, and they all removed into a home arranged according to Western standards of education and comfort.

CHAPTER I

ON February 20th, 1901, the Japanese Times contained the following announcement: " One of the highest and most influential of the whole aristocracy of Japan has decided on having its children (especially its girls) brought up in charge of an accomplished English lady." To which the Japan Daily Mail of February 21st added the following comment: "There is nothing novel in the action taken by Prince Shimadzu unless it be that the lady is to reside with the Prince's family, instead of having a separate home of her own. There can be no doubt, of course, that such a plan must prove more effective for purposes of instruction, but there is not much probability of its being widely adopted, for it entails the necessity of making special arrangements for food, etc., and not many Japanese families are in a position to do that."

On looking back, this suggestion that it was "especially the girls" whom I was to educate causes me amusement, for I was appointed solely to the charge of the sons of this great family; the girls were merely introduced as a piece of journalistic diplomacy. It was long afterwards that I learnt what a commotion my coming had caused, the idea of a woman having anything to do with the sons of a Japanese nobleman being at the time of my arrival almost beyond endurance.

To go back to the beginning. The post one morning brought a letter asking if I would accept a position in Japan if it were offered me. After some hesitation, and relying mainly on my impressions that the Japanese were a delightful people, always laughing and merry, with houses that fell down like a pack of cards when earthquakes came, and were built up again as quickly, I decided to go, regardless of the exact nature of the work, and with no foreshadowing of its enormous responsibilities. The proposal was that I should undertake the care of some orphan Princes, the eldest of whom was a "Daimyo." What that might be I had no notion. I was merely told that a Daimyo was equivalent to a duke.

A talk with Sir Edwin Arnold, however, set me thinking very deeply, and made me keenly interested in my future work. He hinted at there being a certain number of old customs which were still kept up in the houses of Daimyos, and added that it had become necessary to break down many of these owing to recent political developments. Sir Edwin's parting remark made a deep impression on me. c How beautiful it would be," he said, " if you could bring East and West together through the lives of these young noblemen." I often wonder what influence my work really had in this connection, and my justification for writing a book must be that I was the first woman who had ever resided in the family of a Japanese nobleman, particularly in that of the Daimyo of Satsuma.

I started for Japan on December 31st, 1900, under rather strange conditions, as the agreement drawn up by my solicitors had to be left unsigned for two reasons. Firstly, because I had discovered at the last moment that, although I had been told there were three pupils to be educated, two others had been added to my charge, which was alarming, as I did not know if such an addition might be only a preliminary. Secondly, because there seemed to be some difficulty as to what I should be called. Guardian was suggested, but not approved of; Governess was apparently not sufficient, as the children were orphans, and I had to take the place of a parent; Head of the House seemed still less satisfactory. So I set out in some trepidation, with no definite official status and no proper legal settlement. It is, however, interesting to note that in an old diary, kept by a steward of the Prince's household, in which my engagement is entered, Home Instructor is the name assigned to me in the translation.

My voyage out was a long one, taking in all forty-nine days. Owing to the Chinese New Year, which is kept some weeks later than our own, we were delayed in Hong- Kong, waiting for coals.

The first place to touch at in Japan was Nagasaki, where I was kindly entertained by the British Consul.

We spent the next day at Kobe, and there I received my first impressions. I remember seeing a Japanese man, who quite terrified me. He was walking in wooden clogs, such as are used by coolies in muddy weather. They are made of waterproof paper with a place for the toes, after the pattern of our carpet slippers, and are raised on two pieces of wood five or six inches high, which give the wearer quite a tall appearance. This man, who was above the ordinary height, wore a grey wadded kimono, as is usual in cold weather. The wadding is made of floss- silk for the general wearer, but in the case of a poor person a cotton wadding is used, this being much cheaper, but very heavy. This winter kimono is used for a long period and cannot be washed, which is a great drawback, as it is very insanitary. According to a Japanese custom among the lower classes, the man had tucked his arms away for warmth under his kimono, the result being that his sleeves were hanging empty. As he ran towards us they were shaking loosely up and down, and to all appearances he was armless. I flew back, sickened by the sight, to be well laughed at by my fellow passengers, who had lived long in the country.

Another unique sight, and one which I never saw again, gave me a further shock. Many children were playing round the temples, with babies on their backs, as is the universal custom. One girl, however, had tucked her little dog under her kimono, and was carrying it on her back, just as if it were a baby, and as only the head could be seen, I thought at first it was a deformity, and was much horrified. The babies and children did not attract me on this first day; so many had sores on their faces and hands, the cause being, as I afterwards learnt, the need of food more nourishing than rice.

We reached Yokohama on February 17th, early in the morning, and some friends called me up on deck to see Fujiyama, Japan's most illustrious mountain. The sun shining on its snowclad slopes was a wonderful and never-to-beforgotten sight. I remember how, as my heart sank with loneliness and fear, the Psalm kept ringing in my head, " I will lift up mine eyes unto the hills from whence cometh my help " and often did I need it. One of the Japanese passengers told me afterwards that it was a good omen, when arriving, if the sun shone on this mountain. That it certainly was so in my case is seen when I look back upon the seven wonderful years I passed in Japan. In spite of the many difficulties I had to encounter they proved wonderfully happy as a whole, and were quite the most engrossing years I ever spent.

I now had to bid farewell to those under whose care I had been placed. Lord Sandwich, who had been a fellow passenger on the boat, realized in his kind-heartedness that my lot would be a lonely one, and I shall always feel grateful to him for his sympathy and support during his stay in Japan, where he made a tour of some months.

When the Kiatchou pulled up at the quay, I looked eagerly among the spectators, wondering who among them had come to bid me welcome. One of the passengers called my attention to two Japanese gentlemen, saying that they had in all probability come to meet me. Their black frock coats and bowler hats marked them as men of some importance, and as I landed one of these gentlemen immediately handed me his card, with his name, Mr. Hamada, printed in Japanese on one side and English on the other. We shook hands and he addressed me in English, but scarcely a word of it could I understand.

In this first experience, and for many months after, I found the English usually spoken most difficult to understand. For one thing, all the "R's " were pronounced as "L's." During the conversation with these gentlemen I was interrupted by two coolies who brought me a note. They wore dark blue kimonos, with a crest on their back, which denoted that they belonged to a private family. They had, it appeared, been sent by the British Consul to collect my luggage; and it was not long before Mrs. Chalmers, the wife of the Acting Consul, very kindly came to give me a welcome, and invited me to go straight to the Consulate. But as I was informed that we had to leave for Tokio by an early train, and as a luncheon was being given for me with the Princes at twelvethirty, at which the First Secretary of the British Legation and his wife were expected, I was unfortunately not able to accept her hospitality.

I was hurried off in a jinricksha to the station, and upon reaching it was given a first-class ticket to Tokio, which looked so absurdly English with " available on day of issue only " printed on it, that I would fain have kept it and not given it up at my journey's end.

The railway carriage resembled the inside of a tram, with two long seats for twelve persons on each side, and three at the top, in one of which I sat alone, with Mr. Hamada on my left hand. Three long tins covered with cloths or towels were in the carriage as foot- warmers. We exchanged occasional remarks during the journey, but the conversation was a great strain, as I could hardly understand a word said to me. We had one other English or American fellow traveller, to whom Mr. Hamada spoke, and later on two Japanese gentlemen came in. I was bewildered by the constant taking-off of hats, for, not merely on entering and leaving the carriage, but all through the conversation, these gentlemen continually raised themselves and their head-gear. Subsequent experience taught me that the object of a polite Japanese is to be the last to bow: hence the repetition of salutations and the constant taking-off of hats.

The names of the stations were marked up in Japanese characters and in English. The scenery struck me as being not beautiful; rice was the chief production, growing in what looked from a distance like mud or standing water one or two inches deep. Afterwards I got accustomed to these endless rice-fields and loved to see the little hut which was often placed in the middle of fields amongst masses of growing rice. It was a shrine in which the God of Rice could be worshipped, and an image of him seemed to be placed in every temple.

On our arrival at Tokio a carriage met us with another gentleman, who gave his card and proved to be a resident tutor. The carriage was most elaborate, the coachman's livery being decked with gold braid and a crest on his buttons. The footman was a great surprise, and for the first time I grasped the derivation of the word, as literally " a man who runs by the side." He was dressed in a blue tunic with a sun-hat, and had the arms of the house on his back. He was a wonderful runner, going on ahead to pick up any babies in the road, or to clear a blind man out of the way, and occasionally uttering shrill yells as he ran, to warn any obstructing rickshas.

Small-pox was a frequent cause of blindness in the early days before vaccination. Old blind men and women are constantly met with on the roads. These blind folk, however, are put to a very useful occupation. They make splendid masseurs, and are found in most inns and hotels, ready to massage stiff limbs after mountainous climbs or long walks. Their touch is extraordinarily soft, and almost magical for easing pain.

On reaching the house, I noticed that there were several small dwellings adjoining it, and these I learned were inhabited by the attendants. The house itself was an unattractive construction of dark red wood, with a wooden verandah over the entrance. It was situated near the German Legation, and about a quarter of an hour's walk from the British Legation.

When the door was opened, the first person to greet me was Mrs. Whitehead, whom I had known in the Embassy in Berlin, and who was in deep mourning for our beloved Queen Victoria. Standing step-wise behind her were my young charges, four little boys, clad in black suits piped with red, like an English postman's uniform, the regulation dress for the younger boys at the Nobles' School, which they attended. Several gentlemen were also standing in the background, beside a youth who looked about fourteen years old, and was dressed in a dark blue uniform, with two little gold cherry-blossom petals on his collar. This was the Prince, who shook hands with me, after which Mr. Nagasaki, one of the Masters of the Ceremonies at the Emperor's Court, came forward and introduced me to the various gentlemen, the chief being a guardian uncle, who could not speak a word of English, and who looked very disapprovingly at me. Then the four little brothers came up to me; and their bright, attractive faces not only welcomed me but soothed my home-sick heart, and I felt thankful to have them near me.

Mrs. Whitehead then took me upstairs to my bedroom, which had been carefully furnished for me. She told me how anxious the family were that I should be happy and comfortable. The room was a large one, with a Brussels carpet, a nice writing-desk, and various bits of furniture. A little matted room led out of it, occupied by the amah, or maid. The amah, Koma by name, had been especially chosen for my service, because she could speak English; but on the very first remark she addressed to me I found it impossible to understand her, and her ignorance of the language when I spoke to her was expressed in her vacant face. She seemed anxious to please me on that first day of my arrival, but I asked myself silently was there no one who could speak and understand English?

A sudden and overwhelming home-sickness seized me, but it was impossible to yield to it, and I hurried down to tiffin, determined to make the best of everything.

We had to pass through two sitting-rooms in order to reach the dining-room. All the floors were polished parquet. The rooms seemed half furnished, with only a sofa, armchair and six small chairs in each of them, and there were no curtains, pictures or ornaments of any kind. The dining-room was equally bare and had a long, narrow table down the middle.

The Prince and his four brothers sat one side of the table, and on the other side were the Princes' uncle, Mr. and Mrs. Whitehead, Mr. Nagasaki and myself. Each person had a printed menu with the Prince's crest on it, and several men-servants were in waiting. The luncheon was a long affair of endless courses, which the four little boys sat through, occasionally bursting out into laughter, and sometimes amusing themselves by pouring water from one glass into another. Apparently, no servant dared stop them from doing anything, nor venture to correct them. I felt quite anxious over them as they partook of every dish, even sipping wine (a thing they had never done before), and I was not surprised at their unceasing laughter, though they tried to suppress it. The Prince stood up and kindly drank to my health. After luncheon we went through into the first room for coffee, and discussed the work a little. We touched on the legal paper which I had brought unsigned, and it was decided that I should remain on trial for a month to see what the work was like, an arrangement which greatly comforted me, as I felt I could return home as long as the paper was left unsigned.

Soon after the guests left I went to my room to unpack, but on the way up I was taken to see the bath-room which had been built especially for me. How I rued this kind attention later on! I had to go downstairs and to pass through the large play-room, also the billiard-room, and a number of passages, which were very cold. It was a wooden room, containing an ordinary English bath, with two taps, one for cold water, and the other, intended to be for hot water, which merely served for ornament. Besides, there was no outlet for the water to escape!

Never shall I forget my first bath. It was a cause of great excitement to my amah. Having told her to prepare it, I went down and found a round-faced coolie, who instantly prostrated himself on the floor, as was customary on the part of all servants and inferiors of this oldfashioned conservative family. He had a pail, such as we use for cleaning carriages, and was endeavouring to clean the bath, but to all appearances had only succeeded in making it dirty. After this preliminary, with one door open all the time and a bitter wind coming in, he brought two wooden pails full of boiling water. The steam and heat were intense, but the Japanese, I found, like to take their baths almost at boiling point. A doctor told me that by having it so hot the bath acts as a tonic to the skin, and that the use of cooler water in a hot climate is very relaxing. The Japanese, after having boiled themselves, sit in the bathroom without clothes for a short time and fan themselves. On this occasion I dispensed with one pail and had the contents of the other poured into the bath, gradually turning on the cold water, much to their wonder and delight. There was no dish for the soap or sponge, nor any mat to stand on. I afterwards informed Koma, my amah, that I would like these articles, the result being that there arrived a leather case, with gentlemen's hair brushes, powder and hair-pin boxes with metal tops, endless sponges to choose from, and a travelling soap-case. From this first experience of the bath to the end of my stay, if ever I expressed a wish for anything, supreme efforts were made to procure it, my only difficulty at first being to make people understand what I really wanted.

After my bath I had to go down to a five o'clock dinner with the Prince, his brothers, Mr. Nagasaki and Baron Takaki, the Prince's consulting physician, whom I had not met before. He was very kind and genial, and spoke English perfectly, having studied at St. Thomas' Hospital. In his own land he is a great philanthropist, and has founded a hospital, in which he and his eldest son are constantly working for the sick and suffering poor of Tokio. He has also done much valuable work for his country, and for the education of medical students.

This early dinner was to be an ordinary one, such as my young charges would have every evening. The table was spread with a coarse new white cloth; the plates and dishes were of ugly white ware; the spoons and forks were plated, and the glass salt-cellars boasted of no spoons. There were finger bowls filled with hot water, with paper d'oyleys under them. It was quite touching to see the attempt that had been made to conform to English customs. The little boys used big knives and forks, and managed to help themselves neatly from the dishes as they were handed round; but I had many a shock and surprise during that meal, and I saw there was great scope for improvement in their manners.

It greatly puzzled me why the furniture and table service should be of such an ordinary kind. I could not understand the seemingly rigid economy, having heard of the family's great wealth. Later on, I learned the truth. There was a reason for it, and a noble one. The object in adopting this Western education was to get all the best that was possible out of it. What good, they asked, would a luxurious house be to the sons of a great warrior, such as these Princes? Would it help to produce courage and valour? Character could only be beautified by simplicity and denial in daily life. What need to have more than a bare and empty house? There was just one touch of the beautiful for my eye to rest on. In the corner of the room stood two little dwarf plum-trees, in blossom, which made up for any amount of ugly furniture. The Prince's house was renowned for its collection of these wonderful old trees, which are exceedingly difficult to rear. Their height was about two feet, the bark being an exquisite soft grey-green, and the branches covered with pink blossoms. They seemed to me like a peep into fairy-land, and I soon found one placed in my bedroom, showing that my appreciation of them was recognized.

After dinner, sketches of livery were brought from a tailor, and I was asked to select one for the servant who had waited at table. As he was short and dumpy I dreaded the result. I chose a butler's suit, but found they preferred that of a footman, and eventually we decided on a compromise. Mr. Nagasaki then gave me the list of attendant gentlemen, which seemed an endlessly long one, headed by a comptroller of the house, and a treasurer. He told me that Japanese reporters had been continually worrying him for information as to my coming, but that he had kept the date of my arrival unknown until the moment when he had asked the Emperor to excuse him, which had awakened great interest at the Palace. He said he had brought me some very kind messages from the gentlemen in the Court, begging me to believe that I had their sympathy and congratulations on my safe arrival.

Dinner being over we went into the adjoining room, and there I realized for the first time how the eldest brother was accustomed to be treated. An attendant came in, and the Prince was consulted as to my having the use of a carriage. He was grave and silent, and the attendant standing behind his chair spoke for him. Later on I found it was necessary to obtain his permission on any important matter. Strange as it may seem, I never felt that this young Prince was like an ordinary boy of fourteen years of age. In some ways he was a grown-up person. His authority was imperceptibly felt, even by me, a foreigner; and, although he yielded himself to me to educate, and never failed to do all I asked of him, even to giving strict obedience, yet, in a sense, I always felt him to be the Master of the House.

CHAPTER II

I MUST now give a short description of the Prince and his brothers.

On the first day a paper was handed to me with the names and ages of my charges, as follows:

Prince Tadashige Shimadzu, aged 14 years, 5 months.

Baron Tomijiro Shimadzu .. 9 9 ,,

Baron Junnosuke Shimadzu ,, 8 5 ,,

Akinoshin Shimadzu .. 7 2

Yonosuke Shimadzu 6 2

It is to be noted that none of the sons of this celebrated family had been given more than one name. They were not pampered, as are most European princelings, with a string of endless names, for it is not customary in Japan to call a child after any relation or friend.

In the Shimadzu family the word "Tada" was always placed at the beginning of the eldest son's name. This prefix signifies "loyalty," and is given to most of the sons of this princely house, on account of their devoted loyalty to their Emperor. Another name is added to the prefix to distinguish them individually from their ancestors or living relations.

The four youngest boys were given only temporary names which were discarded on reaching years of discretion. The name of the second son, "Tomijiro," signified "Tomi" "rich," and "jiro" "second one," thus indicating the position he held in the family. Before I left this name was dropped, and "Tadamitzu" substituted in place of it. In course of time the third boy's name was also changed to "Tadahiro." As this family is not Imperial, the title of Prince is borne only by the eldest son. The two brothers next to him were created Barons, and the two youngest bore no titles at all. The Prince is, however, closely connected with the Imperial family, and I called him Prince when addressing him, but his brothers and sisters always called him "eldest brother," as is customary in the country.

Precedence of age is of vital importance in all Japanese families. The great veneration in which the eldest son is held is quite astonishing, and he never fails to receive the deepest respect and obedience from all the other members. In our home, indeed, the little brothers soon created an English form of address for their all-important senior, and when speaking of him to me, and to his face, they called him " Big Brother," which name, as years went on, was gradually changed into the abbreviated form of "B.B."

It was a surprise to me to learn the ages of the four little boys, for the youngest did certainly not look more than four years old. I afterwards learnt that the Japanese reckon age by a system different from our own; years are counted by the solar years of the almanac, and should a child be born on the last day of the year, he is said to be two years old the next morning. This is a scheme which would hardly commend itself to any women but the Japanese, to whom age is immaterial, as the colour of her kimono, the mode of doing her hair, and the use and number of her hair ornaments all indicate the age of a married woman. On this point they differ greatly from European women, in whom there is apparently a growing dislike of any style which will make them appear middleaged or matronly.

When first I saw Prince Tadashige I was struck by the sad expression of his countenance. He was exceedingly handsome, with large and beautiful eyes, but there was a look of real care on his brow. His face was oval, a type which, curiously enough, belongs almost exclusively to the nobility, the lower classes being heavyjawed and round-faced. Despite the Prince's youth, he had fully realized the solemnity of his ancestral vow, and, in looking back, I am quite able to understand why he fulfilled his duty so conscientiously in submitting to my education for himself and his brothers. But it was not until later that I realized what an awful contrast that ugly European house, with its bare walls and closed windows, its garden with four walls, its rigid economy, must have been to the dreamy fairy-land garden and house of priceless treasures which he had given up.

He was tenderly interested in his small brothers, and almost paternal as to their training, but to me he seemed at first, and until I understood him better, unapproachable and quite impenetrable.

The second boy, Tomijiro, was so clever a child that I have never met his equal. He was only put under my care for a short time, as the Guardians thought it advisable to give him a different training from his brothers. He needed entirely individual care. Junnosuke, often called "Zun," was a very thin, delicate child, but remarkably wiry. He was full of fun and spirits, with an extraordinary sense of humour, in spite of the old stoical life of the past, in which all expressions of his feelings had been forbidden.

Akinoshin, " Arkey," was of a more meditative and quieter nature; his feelings, which he avoided showing, were deep. He was the strongest built of the brothers, and of a plodding disposition. Yonosuke, or " Tiny," as I nicknamed him in those far-off days, was quite an irresistible little person, very delicate, but full of fun, nothing escaped his notice. The seven years of constant care and watching quite changed his physique.

At first it was a mystery to me why the children had such terribly turned-in feet. I did not know at the time that it was an oldfashioned necessity of the polite world for the feet of a Japanese nobleman to take this position. It tired me more than any other work at the beginning to break the boys of this habit; but it did not take long, for in this, as in everything else, they adapted themselves with marvellous rapidity. It became a second habit to say every few minutes, " Turn your feet out," so much so, that one day, when very over-tired and distraite, I made the same remark to the German Ambassador, Count d'Arco Valley, who, for some absurd reason, happened to sit with his feet turned in when visiting us!

There was another very important member of the family who must not be forgotten. He bore the name of Bogey, and he came to us as a round, warm ball. It was not long before his body grew rapidly in length, but his legs remained dwarfed and bent. Alas! for his nationality he was a dachshund! What a faithful friend was Bogey, in spite of the racial drawback, how learned, how faithful a friend!

I would push aside his long ears and whisper some words to him, probably a message to the Prince or his brothers. Bogey would stand motionless whilst the words were spoken, and wait whilst I put down his long ears again as a covering. Then he would start off in haste to the one whose name I had given him he never made a mistake and would deliver the message by the language of his wise, thoughtful eyes.

Bogey had a great aversion to any signs of parting. He would remain close by the side of his master, the Prince, instinctively knowing that he was going away. When Prince Shimadzu left some years later to go to the Naval College at Etajima, in bidding farewell to Bogey he commanded him to be my special protector, and left me in his charge. The faithful Bogey understood, and from that time he was quite unwilling to leave my side, he followed me everywhere, so persistently that it was commented upon by many people. But he seemed to be strangely restless and sad, as if he had some unknown sorrow, and so it proved to be, for he had said the last farewell to his beloved master. A few days afterwards our dear, faithful Bogey met with an accident, and he was killed.

We all felt his death most deeply, especially the young Princes. They gave him a beautiful little grave in the garden; a bamboo railing was placed round it to fence it off completely, and here they would place minute portions of food, according to custom, to feed his spirit.

CHAPTER III

AS regards the appointment of guardians, there is a great difference between Japan and England. The fact that his parents are living does not prevent a child from being under the complete control of one or more guardians. Amongst the nobility, and, in fact, in the Imperial Family itself, the appointment of a guardian is regarded as a matter of course. As soon as he is a few weeks old a royal prince is placed under the guardian's care in a separate house, and these guardians are sometimes changed before he reaches his majority at eighteen. Thus he may pass through several entirely different hands, and be under the care of men of exactly opposite opinions, which is a very serious matter in his education, and complicates the task of those to whom the training itself is given.

The Prince and his brothers had many guardians, and to my surprise another was subsequently added. As they could not all be consulted, except upon the most important matters, one was especially appointed to act for all. The family was, however, truly blessed in its choice of guardians, who included some of the greatest men in Japan. Prince Oyama, the eminent Field-Marshal; Marquis Matsukata, one of the most eminent statesmen, who has been a great power in the financial world and in his country; Marquis Saigo, whose name is associated with such historical heroism; Admiral Count Kabayama, a man of great repute; and Admiral Count Kamamura, in whose care the present Crown Prince and his brothers were placed as infants. These were the five guardians who were chosen to assist the children's uncle in their up - bringing, at the time of my appointment.

Marquis Matsukata was Acting Guardian. The Emperor of Japan has one or two senior statesmen for whom he sends when any crisis arises; they are known as the Genro, or experienced statesmen. Marquis Matsukata was one of these, and consequently his life was a most absorbing and busy one. I owe him deep gratitude for his patience in listening to my difficulties in the midst of his own very strenuous affairs, and also for his sincere dealings with me, as he always told me openly where he disagreed, and battled for me when he thought I was in the right. I could speak to him perfectly freely, feeling him to be a faithful friend, in spite of his exalted position.

During our many interviews Mr. Nagasaki, a Court councillor, acted as interpreter, and I was also most grateful to him for his untiring part in the work. He never failed to give me help, and his wisdom and tact often made the roughest places smooth.

The Guardians lived far away from the Prince's house and from each other, and in consequence it was difficult to consult them collectively. They were all very busy, and it was hard to arrange for a general meeting. They rarely appeared except on festive occasions, or for matters of vital importance; but at various times I had occasion to seek from them each help which they never failed to give.

That it takes so long to lead up to a subject, owing to the etiquette which must first be gone through, is a very trying Japanese custom. I had often to introduce subjects of which I dreaded the result, and which I approached with an anxious and beating heart, and I found that the suspense added considerably to my difficulties, although I fully realized that the delay arose from a sensitive sympathy with the speaker, and a desire to put one at one's ease before the discussion took place. Marquis Matsukata was a wonderful listener, and when once the subject was opened, he would sit motionless, not missing a word of what I was saying.

Not long after my arrival a cable was sent to Prince Shimadzu from the German Emperor, through Count Wedel, congratulating the Prince on having secured my services, and adding "which I deeply regret to have lost."

In those days such a recommendation was of untold value, and I found this cable a great help. It seemed to complete the perfect confidence of the Guardians, though only time could justify their faith in me. From the very first the German Emperor appeared most interested in my work with Prince Shimadzu' s family. Some time after this cable arrived I had a letter from the Mistress of the Robes, telling me that His Majesty wished to hear all about my work with the Japanese Princes, but I followed the same rule in the Shimadzu family as I had at Potsdam, of silence as to the nature of my work. I wrote only expressing my thanks.

The house seemed full of attendants; I was continually meeting fresh faces. There was an office just opposite the dining-room, where they passed in and out, smoking, talking and drinking tea continually. They resorted to the billiardroom from early morning till late at night, and I often saw the house-boy among the players.

They also took alternate days of service, which considerably complicated matters for me. What I taught a gentleman on Monday needs must be taught over again to a second gentleman on Tuesday. There was a daily visit from the doctor in attendance, whom I discovered administering doses each morning to the Prince and his brothers. When remarking to the amah that I did not know that any of the children were ill, she answered in great surprise, " How could Doctor be so rude a gentleman as not to give Prince and his brothers medicine every day, too rude not to show polite attention? "

The first choice of attendants made by the Guardians was not so fortunate as their later appointments. They were wanting in earnestness, and life seemed all play to them, except for the war-like old attendant, Mr. Ibuski. His sole duties seemed to be the fetching and carrying of clean pocket-handkerchiefs for his young masters. His withered and shrunken body was greatly out of keeping with his warrior spirit. It was quite evident that he hated me. A woman's presence, to say nothing of her interference, was a weakening influence on his feudal lords, who were to be all that was strong and brave in the future, and worthy of the name of their great house.

One day I heard a low voice intoning in the garden, somewhat like the sound of a wail. On looking out I saw the tiny boy sitting perfectly still on the ground, gazing up at his old attendant, with his little face almost as white as marble, while these intonations were being uttered over his head. "What is Mr. Ibuski doing?" I asked my amah, Koma. " He tell brave fight stories to the little gentleman, and tell him to be brave," was the answer. But Mr. Ibuski had a wonderful sense of obedience added to this warlike spirit; he had been told that his young masters were to be educated by me, and in consequence they must be with me. In spite of all his antagonism it was he who trained the youngest child to come to me, when a ruddy-cheeked, blue- eyed foreigner must have been a terror to so young a Japanese child.

In those first days the door used to open and a thin bony hand would thrust this little fellow into the room, in spite of his howls. If he slipped out of the other door by way of escape, he would again be thrust back, with an extra growl from the old man.

As an example of how the attendants regarded my handling of these young boys, I will mention an incident that happened some time after my arrival. I was walking in the garden with two of the children just before the rainy season commenced. The amah had hung up some of my dresses, so as to dry them in the sun before packing them away in tin boxes. I noticed one of the gentlemen call the children to him in quite an excited and anxious voice. On their return I asked what was the matter, and was told that the gentlemen had advised them not to walk near the clothes-line, as it would make them weak if they went near to where a woman's clothes were hanging. The second set of attendants chosen by the Guardians were most earnest workers, and in looking back, I realize how much they helped me in the work, especially the head gentleman, Mr. Hirata. Not that we always understood one another how could we when our customs and ideas were so totally different? It was hard to convince them that a change for the Prince and his brothers would be for their good, but if they once believed it to be advantageous they would fight for it, in spite of having to introduce Western ideas.

Unfortunately, at the beginning I made many changes, which all unknown to me affected some of the retainers, as, for instance, in the matter of the children's clothes. They seemed to be worn and cast away indiscriminately, in fact, they were scarcely used; the reason being that such important children could not wear the same clothes for very long. I had ordered two suits of uniform for everyday use and two suits for best, and by thus restricting the clothes I had unconsciously injured some of the attendants' families, as it had been the rule for all cast-off clothes to be handed over to their children, which was quite a natural and sensible proceeding, considering what small salaries they receive. I was not informed of this at the time, but I felt an atmosphere of disapproval all around me, as the attendants always had the Prince's ear, and I found they were often able to influence him against me in those early days when none of us understood each other. Gradually, however, they began to be interested in European clothes for themselves, and I used constantly to be asked to choose materials for suits, neckties, and even socks and underclothes. I remember a servant bringing some patterns of under-garments one afternoon at tea on a tray, and asking me which colour would be best, much to the amusement of some of my visitors.

There was another thing which I wished to change for the benefit of my charges. I noticed that they showed no interest in the lives of their attendants; no matter how hard they worked, their young masters never thought that they could be tired. Nor did the children ever express thanks. Added to this, they showed no generous instincts of giving money to the poor and suffering; so entirely ignorant were they of poverty and sorrow that it seemed impossible for them to realize either in fact, they had a merely selfish outlook on life. Everyone was, as it were, a walking-stick, to be used and put away in a corner when not wanted. What opportunity, I asked myself, had they of self-denial? How could I make them independent, unselfish, kindhearted and grateful? On the other hand, if their characters should develop these virtues, what scope would there be in the future for all these endless attendants? What work would be left for them to do? Again, how could these children be generous and self-denying if they had no money of their own to spend, and if shopping and buying were prohibited? How could they feel for sufferers if pains and sorrows were kept from them, and if they never mixed with the outside world? The attendants had hitherto done all the shopping for them and had given money in their names to all charitable institutions and deserving cases; reformation in these things seemed to spell revolution.

The Guardians, however, came to my aid in these as in many other matters. They stood by me for the good of the children's characters, and proved themselves wise, patient and tactful. A great change took place. The Prince and his brothers visited hospitals, and were given money to spend, and allowed to go out shopping. No show of outward dissatisfaction appeared on the part of the gentlemen; all was stoically accepted by them. Smiles were still seen, but the hearts of these faithful men ached lest their Princes and young masters should lose the dignity of their position. They were silently resenting the changes all the time, and influenced my charges so that they were unwilling these innovations should be carried out. I saw it would be a fight to the finish if my work were to succeed. This state of affairs was very puzzling to my European eyes. Here was a young lord, whose attendants would prostrate themselves on the ground, who was considered too " almighty '; to approach, and whose word meant law, completely under the control of these very men, doing as he was bid or, perhaps, as a better word, doing as he was asked. What contradiction it all seemed!

The fact also of not speaking Japanese made my work very difficult. The children would suddenly tell me that they were all going out, two carriages would appear at the door in readiness, and without any further notice they would drive away, accompanied by attendants. I had no means of discovering where they had gone or when they would return, and had to wait at home all day, hourly expecting them. I brought this difficulty to the Guardians, who arranged that in future a written notice of their plans should be always given to me.

Sometimes I would suddenly be given a Japanese card, and go down to find a visitor waiting in the drawing-room. I could not read the card. It might be a duke or it might be a shopman they all presented cards. I would send for Koma, and in her broken and limited English, regardless of the presence of the visitor, she would say, "This is a big gentleman, or a rich gentleman, or a big prince; " or " Oh! he is office-gentleman, he is not so big." It was a painful experience! Added to my other difficulties a constant stream of visitors kept arriving in jinrickshas, to visit the gentlemen of the household, which puzzled me until I discovered that the calls were made on the Prince, and that the duties of the attendants required their receiving such polite attentions in his name. The rooms were sometimes dense with smoke, and little Japanese teacups (with no handles) were to be seen in every nook and corner when the visitors had departed. After a time we instituted a reception room, set apart entirely for this purpose, but in those early days the impression I received was that the house resembled an inn all passers-by looked in and stayed for a talk! The visits were often of long duration and, except in my own room, privacy was impossible. Besides these visitors, ceaseless school friends came to the house out of school hours, supplemented by children belonging to the attendants. At first the sight of a foreigner, especially one with blue eyes and fair hair, produced peals of laughter: I must confess that those days had their minor trials! The office seemed to have a great attraction for the children while they were still strangers to me, and I used mentally to compare it to a spider's web, in which my charges were the flies.

Sometimes when I was with the eldest son a gentleman would come in, and would deliver a long message, the purport of which I never knew. The same difficulty arose when the Prince had friends. Two or three school-boys would perhaps appear suddenly, and I would not know who they were, as no names or introductions were given to me; they might be young Princes of importance, or on the other hand they might be quite undesirable acquaintances. They would all talk together, and not a word could I understand, but I felt the influence for good or bad on the children after they had left, and the choice for them of good friends weighed heavily on my mind.

CHAPTER IV

IT became only too evident in the course of time that I must have an interpreter. On my first search for one, some of the Japanese ladies (and they are not partial to scandal) warned me against employing any girl who was "high-collared," which, as a word corresponding to our epithet "fast," amused me greatly. Later on I found it constantly used, and that when applied to a man it indicated that he was worthless and without industry or a sense of duty.

As I depended entirely on my interpreter in the daily interviews with the attendants, this was a difficult post to fill, and I had many changes during the seven years of my stay there.

I often enjoyed the idle prattle of my girl interpreters, who, through necessity, were as many as their tales were varied. One of them was much attached to her church, whose vicar was a Japanese. He was also, incidentally, her godfather, and I think the two facts resolved themselves into one equation! It was, according to my informant, a custom of her church for converts receiving baptism when grown up to be allotted god-parents, and in view of the fact that quite young men often exercised this authority over quite young girls it would seem that the baptized made their own choice in the appointment! It is hardly necessary to comment on the abuse this might, and no doubt did, lead to, for the god-parents had considerable authority over their wards.

In the particular case I am citing (and I heard of the practice only from the one source), my interpreter's god-father was an elderly married man, whose advice she sought before taking the smallest step. At the time of her employment with me her god-father was away in India on a several months' visit, his mission, as she described it, being slightly discomposing to my mind. " He has gone, not only for religion," she told me, " but also because he feels sorry for the people in India. He does not think it right that they should not govern themselves and be an independent people, as we are. He is going to give them his advice." Such were her remarks, which, if noticed in political circles, might have caused trouble though it is fully possible that the wonderful British rule in India impressed this Japanese cleric even to the point of conversion when he encountered it first hand.

Japanese women and girls are exceedingly irresponsible in the remarks they make and views they express. I have heard quite heated discussions arise among a Japanese " hen " party on the advantage New Zealand would be to the Japanese, one argument being that their nation is growing so fast and" where can it spread to if America and Australia won't let us in? We must get a big colony of our own to put our people in." New Zealand is an ideal spot to the Japanese; they like the people, and they are always enthusiastic over their visits. It was certainly so with the Navy. On the return of the Japanese Squadron which had visited New Zealand and various other countries the officers could not speak warmly enough of their reception. They seemed to love the people and enthused over the scenery, wealth and produce of the country.

Tokio has an excellent school for girls, established by Miss Tsuda, a very clever and delightful lady who has done a great work among her pupils, and my best interpreters undoubtedly came from her school. These girls gave me an insight into the life of a Japanese student. After leaving school their one aim appears to be that of improving themselves. The money earned is almost always devoted to fees, to enable them either to perfect themselves in modern languages, or to go through some training preparatory to a profession. They will forego all kinds of pleasures and entertainments and even necessities for this purpose; no work is too menial, if only they can earn sufficient money for their object.

This life of self-denial does not appear to be exclusively confined to girls; the lives of all Japanese students are very hard and earnest, and there is much to be admired and honoured in them.

As regards my interpreters, my heart does not go out in gratitude to them all; some added greatly to my difficulties at times. In the first place, it was contrary to their national characteristics to speak one's mind openly, regardless of whom it might hurt or offend. I often saw a look of horror on my interpreter's face when I had any unpleasant matter to discuss; and I noticed that after speaking long and animated sentences to be interpreted the result would be summed up in two or three Japanese words. One felt completely in their power and at their mercy. Most of the interpreters seemed afraid of the attendants, and from the very beginning of our interviews I generally felt that they put themselves on the side of these gentlemen against myself and my views. The answers received to my questions were often impolite and annoying, owing, I believe, to a wrong interpretation: it needed plenty of self-control to sit calmly through those daily talks!

The Prince was a good billiard player, and even his young brothers could make a fairly good score. Billiards are a very favourite game with the Japanese and many of them are skilful players; the Prince used to hold billiard matches for his attendants twice a year in which he and all the gentlemen competed, and for which numerous prizes were given. I soon realized, however, that this incessant billiard playing was very detrimental to the moral influence of the household; practising for these competitions caused the attendants to waste a great deal of time, and eventually billiards ceased to be played in the European house, and the matches took place in the large Japanese house.

Those early days were very anxious ones, as I soon realized that I had been given the care and responsibility of these boys and was unable to take complete control of them. It seemed as if things never could be righted, and I have often, on looking back, thought it marvellous how my many difficulties were gradually overcome.

In those first days I was much oppressed by loneliness, and watched anxiously for the arrival of the mails, which then took forty- five days via Suez there was no Siberian Railway at that time. Such belated home news was an unpleasant introductory experience.

Never hearing English spoken, and not being able to understand one word of Japanese, was also a considerable strain. I had brought several letters of introduction and had hoped to present them, but within a short time the inadvisability of doing so revealed itself. I was a stranger, the first European woman who had ever resided in the family of a Japanese nobleman, and if I had visited many English families I might easily have been suspected of gossiping, which is abhorrent to the Japanese mind. I therefore resolved to wait, and to lead a secluded life, devoting all my time to the work itself, until I became better understood and could feel more trusted.

Day by day fresh difficulties presented themselves, particularly in regard to the housekeeping, which almost overwhelmed me. Turn where I might some change was needed. The fire-grates were all rusty, the mantel- shelves and windows in a terrible condition; in fact, this "home " had the appearance of a vacated house, and the cold of it was appalling, without so much as a strip of carpet in any of the sitting-rooms.

There also seemed no sense of time in the establishment, and my first move was to institute a dinner-bell. That this innovation was regarded as an important one by the attendants is proved by the fact that I discovered later that it had been entered in the diary kept by the attendants for important records and dates. What excitement this bell caused, and how strange was the use to which it was subjected! What with the language difficulty and the want of punctuality, the poor bell rang by fits and starts, sometimes pealing loudly so early as to awaken us long before it was time to get up, and at other times ringing as we sat at meals. I tried to teach the house-boy to lay the cloth for meals, but found it quite impossible to get him to do the same thing in the same way twice. He was extraordinarily quick in picking up English, and in all other matters, but he was a Japanese. When you visit the pottery works of the country you will never find two pots exactly alike; there are no pairs of ordinary mantelpiece vases like our own. Tea-cups, saucers, plates, even of the cheapest ware, have varied patterns on each. The Japanese artistic nature admits no duplicate; and I found this characteristic through all the house work. To fit a teatray with tea-pot, cups and milk jug placed in an orthodox style was at first an impossibility. The tea-pot would arrive, followed by milk as an after-thought. Pieces of toast came one by one, butter had no connection with bread but a smile invariably accompanied them. There is something refreshing in living in a land of smiles, some of which, however, in those early days I did not understand. When anything was broken the culprit would hand it to me with a smile, and I felt, " What impertinence! ' Later on I learned that this was a smile of politeness, very often the mask of penitence. Generally the potbreaker was sorry.

I found it necessary to make a change in the hours for meals, and arranged both breakfast and the evening meal later; I also insisted on a longer time being spent at the table. The way in which those children bolted their food was quite extraordinary, especially at breakfast. Doubtless this originated from the Japanese custom of hasty meals, for, except on feast days, to sit long over one's food is regarded as a great waste of time, and the more quickly it is eaten the more virtue attaches to the partaker of the meal the children spoke as if it were wrong to eat slowly.

At almost every meal, in addition to other dishes, there was beefsteak, provided as a concession to my national tastes. To a Japanese novice European food is represented solely by beefsteak, and the attendants apparently believed it to be a necessity for me wherever we went.

The meals themselves consisted of many courses, after the style of a hotel, and might have been cooked by a French chef; but they were most unwholesome for such young children, and I found it necessary to alter their diet at once, and to give them light, simple food. This as it happened was rather difficult to manage: I found large quantities of provisions had been ordered every week, such quantities as to be almost beyond belief. These, under the new arrangement, would no longer be required, and in consequence there were fewer perquisites for the kitchen, which caused great dissatisfaction in certain quarters. It was soon after this that I received my first anonymous letter in which I was warned that it was not safe for me to go out alone, and was also told to avoid walking near bushes and hedges. The paper, writing and English were all such poor specimens of their kind as to make me suspect that it came from the kitchen, and I laid no great stress upon it, in fact I did not mention it to anyone, except to my amah, Koma, in whose presence I tore it up, declaring it was nothing but nonsense.

I instituted drawing-room tea, and this soon became a very happy hour for us all. We managed to procure some diminutive chairs of a most fascinating kind, in which the merry little people would sit by my side, and as time went on they vied with each other as to which one should occupy the seat nearest to me. In the course of time their big brother joined us, and soon applied himself to handing the cakes and tea to me, and teaching his brothers to do likewise.

As for the conversation, it seemed as if the children learned to speak English in their dreams. Their quickness was amazing, and I was very soon able to read aloud to them. Later, when they could understand it, we read the " Jungle Book," and they nearly went mad over it, and wished me to procure (i< Rikki-Tikki-Tavi," as another member of the family. " The Big Brother" had a piano brought in, and they soon learnt to sing all the old nursery songs. Evening after evening we sang and shouted to our hearts' content. They sang well, too, which is not easy for Japanese; European airs are totally different from the weird, monotonous music of their own songs, which sound so tuneless to us on first hearing them.

One small difficulty quickly revealed itself in the use of the word " boy." How was I to explain that there was a second meaning to it besides that used in the East for the house servant? If one of the children had done anything extra well, I used naturally to exclaim, "Good boy! " and would suddenly see a look of surprise on their faces. On one occasion, I remember, when I used the expression to the eldest, a look of resentment instantly arose, as though I had insulted him. It was quite a long time before I could make the matter clear, but eventually it was fully understood.

On the other hand, I was much puzzled by the indefinite way in which the word " San " was used after the name of a person, in place of Mr., Mrs., Master and Miss. There was no distinguishable difference; a visitor was announced by name, followed by ;c San " only, and it remained to be seen who might be awaiting one in the drawing-room. This custom must produce complications even for the Japanese, and for foreigners it is a most awkward one. I remember hearing of some foreign lady who, on the death of her husband, was confronted with letters relating to her own death. The news had come that one of them had died, but apparently the word " San " did not clearly prove which! Among the nobility the word " Sama " is used for all sexes in place of " San," and princes and princesses have the word " Miya " attached to the end of their names.

Shopping was a disappointment to me at first, because the shopmen all came to the house, a most trying custom to an Englishwoman, whose love of sales reveals the joy it is to handle and examine a hundred arid one things before selection. The Japanese nobility did not shop; they were too important to be among the bargain throng. However, I soon started on European lines, and a few days after my arrival went out shopping, accompanied by an attendant and amah.

My first question was, " Where are the shops? ': and I felt greatly disappointed when our jinrickshas suddenly pulled up at a small Japanese house, with an open-fronted room by way of shop-window. The china goods which were for sale there were spread on the ground, and one or two

Japanese girls were sitting outside, ready to show their wares. A few streets away there were shops more like those we are used to at home; but experience soon taught me that the really beautiful objects for sale (the work of individuals) were not to be purchased from any mere store or shop. In quite obscure places one might come across a poor man working day and night at a single object, using all his artistic craft and putting his whole soul into it. There is very little chance of being confused by quantities of different wares, as things are brought out one by one for inspection.

When speaking to these shopmen (or, for that matter, to the attendants also) the extraordinary difficulty of getting any information at times required much patience. A question from me generally resulted in long and audible selfcommuning, and on asking Koma in despair to obtain an answer for me, she would remark, "Not ready yet, they are thinking." The pricing of things also worried me, lest I should spend too much, but Koma often interpreted the attendant's remarks to me as meaning " He says, no matter how big money, you buy what you like." It was rather a relief to be told that!

The barbers' shops have a long black and white sign-pole over the entrance, and as they are all exactly alike, it is difficult to distinguish one from the other. A friend of mine, whose serious illness in Japan necessitated her hair being shaved off, took her own beautiful auburn hair, upon her recovery, to a hairdresser to be made into a long tail. She was asked to call for it in a few days' time. Alas! when in quest of her hair, she could not distinguish the barber's shop, not having noted the name. It took her some hours to find her coiffure, and when eventually, after long " hunting of the hare," the auburn locks were presented to her, she was very disappointed with the mode of dressing. To console her, however, the hairdresser deftly wound the hair into a chignon and placed it on top of his own bald head, asking her with enthusiasm to note how well it looked when actually worn. Strange to say, this did nothing to convince her!

When I first entered the china shops I felt I could buy everything I saw, but it did not take long for me to realize the commonness of cheap ware, and to resist the attraction of its blue colour. I have often been amused, since my return from Japan, to see the various Japanese articles that are ignorantly used as ornaments in English drawing-rooms, and the cotton materials, which are used exclusively in Japan for bathing purposes, often covering chairs and sofas, and hanging as curtains. How strange this must appear to Japanese eyes! On the other hand, I have often suppressed laughter over the strange selection of European hats in Japan. I think one of the funniest sights I saw in this way was at a garden-party given by Count Okuma. Among the guests was a Japanese gentleman dressed in complete Japanese costume, who wore a high silk hat stuck on the back of his head, and reminded me of the " mad hatter " in " Alice in Wonderland." I suppose the misuse of clothes and miscellaneous commodities is pretty equal as between our two countries.

I had been asked to furnish my bedroom in such a way as to make it absolutely European in every respect, even to the minutest details. Consequently, when it was finished everyone wanted to see it, and I used to love to show it.

The Japanese have a great charm in making one feel thoroughly satisfied with one's own possessions, but at the same time they are wonderfully observant. My visitors were mostly gentlemen, many of whom were statesmen and ministers, yet, although burdened with their country's cares, they could take the keenest interest in every detail. Everything was carefully noted.

Besides the actual furniture itself, they seemed interested in all the usual, personal details such as handkerchief and veil- cases, which had been given me by several friends; and even my nightgown-case lying on the pillow did not escape their attention. From the long camphor-wooden box, which I kept for housing furs in the rainy season, to the hangers in my cupboard for coats, everything excited their curiosity; and my amah was often consulted by other amahs belonging to the houses of the nobility. She loved, in her turn, to display all my possessions, and it was a shock to me to discover one day that my nightgown and handkerchief -cases were missing, and that she had allowed them to be sent to a shop to be copied.

The monograms on these cases were embroidered in old English characters, which had evidently been taken for a curious design, and I was told that they were being copied exactly, excepting that other coloured silks had been chosen. I wondered greatly on whose pillow my duplicate nightgown- case would lie, and whose handkerchiefs would hold the case bearing my initials. Verily I was open to scandal!

CHAPTER V

THERE was a nice large garden surrounding the house, but the grass was terribly dry, and there were no flower-beds. This garden, like the furniture, was designed for the benefit of the boys; it was intended solely for recreation, and attached to it was a large gymnasium ground with a vaulting horse and swing. One morning, looking out of my window, I saw a number of little old women studded about the lawn; their heads were tied up with blue cotton towels, matching their faded blue kimonos, and they were on their knees, laughing and chatting. What could they be doing, I asked myself. It transpired that they were the gardeners; each had a pair of shears, and they were cutting and weeding the grass. It was, I learned afterwards, nothing out of the common, as gardening is considered to be old women's work in Japan, and although it seemed as if they were at play, and as if no work could possibly be accomplished, I discovered that I had judged them wrongly. The effect of their labours was almost magical. Observation taught me that this extraordinary attitude towards work is a national characteristic, and that all workmen, on the roads, in the buildings, or in other constructions, always appeared to be idling away their time, or dreaming and neglecting their duties. When the elevated railway in Tokio was being erected, I used to watch and wonder if it would ever get finished; but I soon learned that, although the progress appeared to be slow, the results were good, and that after having despaired of ever seeing the end of a work, one would wake up one morning to find it suddenly and unexpectedly completed. It was so in the case of these old gardeners. Their pay was a mere pittance, but they were apparently able to afford the luxury of unlimited tea and tobacco, although I imagine that these were often their only substitute for a meal.

Sometimes the children used to play in the garden, and it often disturbed me to see them and their young friends catching dragon-flies, which flew about in quantities. It was the only " boys' fun " I ever recall as bordering on cruelty in Japan; otherwise they were kind to all animals, and collected butterflies with much earnestness and care. But the dragonfly suffered at their hands. It seemed piteous to see this beautiful coloured creature, whose life was in any case of such short duration, captured and tortured by having its fairy wings pulled out. It was, perhaps, a form of sport which corresponded to Western boys' love of bird-nesting.

We spent our evenings in playing games, and I taught the Prince to play chess, which soon became very popular. My pupils made very clever players too, and often beat their teacher. The Japanese game of chess, " Shogi," is far more complicated than ours. Each player has twenty pieces of flat wood, with Japanese characters engraved on both sides of them. To " crown " these pieces, one reverses them, and the game, as it is played, can never result in stalemate. After a few lessons I abandoned it, leaving the Prince to play with his brothers, as it proved altogether too complicated to master without giving strenuous attention to it. There was also a game called " Go," which they keenly enjoyed. This has a thick wooden board marked out in many squares, and is played with round, flat, black and white pebbles in great quantities; the worst player is given the black stones, as they are slightly easier to use. One game may be prolonged indefinitely, and when bedtime came the children often left the board with strict orders that the pebbles should not be disturbed, so as to continue the game the next day, and even then there was not always time enough to get it finished. One constantly saw two men engaged for hours at it, sitting on the mats of shops, houses, or inns, in absolute silence.

One of my pupils' characteristics was that they would be playing hard at some game, with high enthusiasm, during the greater part of perhaps two days, after which they would drop it entirely. Of fireworks, however, they never tired, especially those which may be let off indoors, their noise never failing to let you know of their proximity.

Love of change was a Japanese characteristic which forced itself on my notice everywhere. I believe this craving for continual variety accounts to a large extent for the waves of pro- and anti-foreign spirit which frequently flood the country from one end to the other.

Bedtime had to become a fixed hour, and this was a grave necessity, for I found these little people needed training in sleeping. As "men of importance," they had been accustomed to get up and go to bed when the spirit moved them. I remember that the first morning, on opening the bedroom door, I encountered a blaze of electric light, and that when I asked the reason, I was told, <c the young masters wished it." The three youngest had slept with all the lights up in their rooms, and also all the blinds up, ready

for the early dawn. They rose with the lark, and consequently were tired out before the day's work began. It is most exceptional in this land of earthquakes and fires to find any person sleeping in the dark, but the children gradually became accustomed to it. They were of a nervous, imaginative nature, like most of those born to high estate, and I had to humour them by gradually decreasing the number of burners to one light, and afterwards by replacing that by a candle, and later by a night-light, till finally they became willing to sleep entirely in the dark, excepting in summer, when the little fairy fireflies which they kept in cages by their bedside came to their aid.

Often when my work was finished I would go upstairs and look at the children as they slept, and it helped me in my loneliness, for the evenings were very solitary. They looked so sweet with their closely-cropped heads of hair, in little pink and white pyjamas which I had made for them. I could often have taken the tiny one up in my arms. From the very first day of my arrival, however, I adhered to the Japanese custom of never kissing them. The Japanese never kiss each other, they merely bow, and it seemed wiser not to introduce such foreign customs lest they might be misunderstood. In spite, however, of my showing but little outward affection, I felt that my "motherly " influence drew them towards me, and that they felt Jt imperceptibly. Once, later on, when reading aloud one of Mrs. Gatty's "Parables from Nature," the youngest boy surprised me by seizing my hand and kissing it. A friend had once visited me, whom I had kissed as a matter of course, an action which had caused a burst of laughter from the children, who afterwards asked why she had licked me! This was the only kiss the child had come across, and yet in his quick perception he knew it was a mark of affection.

Apropos of kissing, an incident in the RussoJapanese war (that time which happily reminds us that warfare on both sides can be conducted by honourable men) is worth recording.

To the astonishment of a Japanese commander, one of his soldiers brought into his presence a Russian prisoner whose hands were tied.

"What has the prisoner done to deserve such treatment? "

"Sir he tried to bite me."

The explanation of this was that the prisoner was so grateful to his captor for the tea, good food and many cigarettes, etc., which had been given him, that he had insulted the Japanese by trying to kiss him!

How to start in teaching these young boys to speak English seemed a nightmare. I taught the eldest brother in the garden out of school hours, and found he had already studied the language at school for some time. They also learnt many words at meals for example, I would hold up a spoon and give its name, and they would repeat it after me. It was wonderful how quickly they learned to speak, but for a long time it was only parrot talk. If, when teaching them a word, I thoughtlessly made some remark, it became part of the name of the object shown. On one occasion I remember teaching them to say "tea-cup," and without thinking, I added, "Sit up, don't fidget," the result being that the word "tea-cup" became almost an impossibility for them to learn. Nothing would convince them that "tea-cup-situp-don't-fidget" was not its name! As a diversion one evening I introduced "Animal Grab," thinking that with their extraordinary quickness I could easily make them grasp it, but to my horror I found it was not only man's language that differed from our own, but that of the animals as well. The "miew" of a cat to them was a totally different sound, and so was the "moo" of a cow. This was a revelation, and eventually it became a great amusement as time went on for us all to compare our animal languages.

The youngest boy, "Tiny," was unusually silent, but did not on that account shut his ears. One day he suddenly surprised me, after banging a door extra loud, by saying, "Pargum." He afterwards invented degrees of "Pardon." After a small misdemeanour he would calmly look up and say, "Little pargun;" a more serious one demanded a "Big pargun."

It was a great help at the beginning to write notes to the Prince in the house, and as we found this a much easier method than speaking, it became a means of our better understanding of one another. I did the same later on with some of his school friends, who were naturally silent and reserved, indeed, I believe it would have been almost impossible to get into touch with them had it not have been for these notes. I well remember how joyfully I hailed one small missive which contained the words: "Are you husbanded? " I felt the writer had begun to take interest in my life, and was a little more in touch with the " foreign lady." It must have been a shock to receive the answer to this bold question in the negative, for in those days it was taken for granted in Japan that a girl was married when she attained the designated age, unless there was some screw loose. I often wondered what they thought I was lacking in!

Full of zeal for the progress of my work, I resolved to learn colloquial Japanese myself, and started by getting my amah to teach me the " Thank you " of daily life. Having learnt it perfectly, I started practising it on my ricksha coolie. Horror of horrors! Never should so great a lady use such language to a coolie! That "Thank you" was only for the noble young gentlemen. Here was an eye-opener, and I quickly found that even these two simple words had several forms of expression. " Most dangerful," as the little amah expressed it, were my early attempts at the language. Afterwards, as I have said, I was provided with an interpreter, although the start was not propitious, for she translated the Japanese quite literally, without giving me any help or guidance as to their customs and intentions.

As an example, the wife of one of the Emperor's chamberlains paid me a visit, during which she adhered to the strictly polite Japanese practice of depreciating her home and family and all that appertained to it, and praising and exalting all that belonged to me. She invited me to tea with her, and my interpreter passed on the invitation in the following manner: "Madam asks you to come and clean her house by your bright presence; her house very dirty, her home no use, she have ugly children, please you come and clean it." To describe my consternation and anxiety over this remark is not easy: I believed she had asked me to come and do some house-cleaning for her. With an unsigned agreement in my mind, and the anticipation of a possible increase of work, this suggestion was most disquieting. Many a laugh did we afterwards have over this misunderstanding.

Apropos of this polite depreciation, a Japanese diplomat, apologizing in a letter for his wife's absence, referred to her as his " thorny wife." On another occasion, when I noticed the absence of a big fat coolie, whose daily duty it was to polish the floor, the interpreter informed me that he had " gone back to his Mama" meaning to say he had left and returned to his province!

There are many words in the Japanese language with more than one meaning. On one occasion, for instance, the wife of one of our diplomats received a message through her interpreter to the effect that " the master is returning from Yokohama bringing with him a concubine." The real message was, " bringing with him a joint of meat for dinner!"

Later on, when the boys' English improved, I used to make them sit in a row opposite me after breakfast every morning, and I taught them one or two words by heart. I had a calendar with quotations *upon it, and selected the following words:

"Little self-denials, little honesties, little passing words of sympathy, little nameless acts of kindness, little silent victories over favourite temptations, these are the silent threads of gold, which, when woven together, gleam out so brightly in the pattern of life that God approves."

I think it took us nearly a year to learn and to understand the meaning of this, but eventually they grasped it. To my surprise they would over and over again bring the quotation into practice, repeating it to me in a whisper. If I happened to do any kindness, I have known them pinch my elbow, asking if I had done it because of those words.

Sometimes their questions were very difficult to answer, particularly as I had been told not to mention Christianity. One day, when protecting a persecuted cat, one of them suddenly said, " Do you love that cat because you are a Christian? " Good works sank very deeply into the hearts of these Japanese boys, whose ancestors had lived a life of silence and meditation.

It was not only in language that we differed, but our ideas and customs continually clashed. Take, for instance, the Prince's reception of gifts, which he daily received from the men of his province and others. An attendant would carry these in and present them with a bow; the Prince would never look at them, made no comments and expressed no thanks, giving me the idea of gross ingratitude. It was only at a later time that I discovered that it was considered impolite to examine a present, at any rate in the presence of the giver. Most puzzling, also, it was to see his reception of a visitor. There was no gracious offering of a chair, no expression of pleasure at the visit, just a bow and dead silence. In my ignorance, I misunderstood and misjudged everything. As regards the gifts themselves, there is something very fascinating in the way such presents are given. I remember on receiving my first gift I felt quite unwilling to open the parcel, for it was wrapped up in the whitest of paper, and tied with the prettiest red and white string; accompanying it was a piece of paper folded at the top, like a three-cornered note, and secured to the parcel by a funny little bit of dried fish. Some Japanese writing was on it, but whether it was my name or the donor's I never discovered. Every gift is wrapped up in this way, and it must indeed be an arduous work on an occasion when several are presented; but it undoubtedly gives one a charming impression that much thought and pains have been bestowed by the donor.

Those early days presented many strange problems to me, and still more, I fancy, to the young Prince. When I first went there the men of his province would have been quite pained to sit in his presence, and would have looked upon their young master as lacking in self-respect and dignity if he had expressed any welcome, pleasure, or thanks. How different from the present regime in Japan, where my former charge is now quite one of the most gracious and hospitable of hosts!

The breaking through this wall of reserve was in itself alone an enormous undertaking. It needed to be done so gradually, and when once achieved the result also needed a certain amount of control, especially in the case of the youngest brothers. Difficulties at once arose of an opposite character, for the boys, having been restrained for so long, readily adopted a natural manner, and sometimes expressed their feelings too openly.

Peals of laughter rang through the house, and at times tears were also shed, which needed checking lest this might be considered common and plebeian. Many a time the immoderate laughter had to be checked by a severe rebuke, and I found it necessary to record tears in a mark-book, to which I gave the name of the "crying book." This book worked magically, and stopped many a howl.

The introducing of Western customs was also very difficult in regard to the Prince. I can still recall the look of almost antagonism and fear on the children's faces when I mildly asked their eldest brother to ring the bell for me. " Fancy asking Big Brother to ring the bell! " was their remark, which of course made it more difficult for him to carry out my request. Sometimes attendants straight from his province would come to pay their respects, and would lie prostrate on the ground before him. All this needed to be changed gradually, and how was I to do it without lessening his greatness or wounding their susceptibilities? Great tact and discretion were required on my part, and the patience with which the attendants bore the necessary innovations was quite wonderful.

One of the most drastic changes took place towards the end of the first twelve months in the dismissal of certain police guards outside the gate. I was anxious that my charges should go in and out of school as ordinary pupils, without the necessity of acknowledging salutes; consequently the guards were dismissed and the little sentry-boxes remained empty. This was beyond the endurance of some of the retainers, who did their best to convince me of the necessity for guarding the Princes, and also for ensuring my own safety.

CHAPTER VI

THE Prince and his brothers daily attended the Gaksuhin, or Peers' School, which although it bore this name, was not exclusively confined to the nobility, some of the attendants' sons being also admitted. This arrangement placed the various pupils in a somewhat strange position, for although there was the usual bon camaraderie within the school, the necessary reverence to sons of the nobility had always to be kept up out of school hours.

The elasticity of this unique system is remarkable. When, for instance, the present Crown Prince entered this school at the age of seven years, he and his attendants were duly received in the morning by the elected Principal, who was then General Nogi. The ceremony proper to the opening of the new term was held; a proclamation from the Emperor was read as usual, and each pupil passed in front of His Imperial Majesty's photograph, making his obeisance. Twelve little boys had been especially chosen among the princes and nobility as class companions to the Crown Prince. After the opening ceremony, they were all conducted to the classroom and placed in the hands of a teacher, who addressed them all as ordinary pupils, explaining to them the rules of the school, and putting them upon a common footing. But although for the time being the honours of the young Prince were waived, the awe inspired by the royal presence existed for a long time afterwards, and I remember once, when going over the school, being asked by one of the pupils with bated breath if I had seen the desk at which the present Emperor used to sit, and being told that it had been left vacant ever since as a mark of respect.

In those days the President of the Gaksuhin was given complete control over the school, and this always seemed to me to be a great drawback to the scholars, as fresh elections were made and the whole tone of the school was continually changed with each President. I had hard work to steer my charges through a safe course. The school, being founded on military principles, often proved too hard a discipline for the sons of the nobility; many of the pupils had inherited delicate constitutions from their noble parents, and the i severe military training greatly taxed their strength. There was no regular daily exercise, as in our schools, to train the pupils into good walkers, but a long excursion would suddenly be arranged without any preparation having been made for it. I found that these expeditions often knocked the children up, and desired them daily to walk to and from school, notwithstanding the rainy season. But many objections were made to the suggestion. Umbrellas and mackintoshes were forbidden, and only thick military coats with hoods for their heads were allowed, which were very unsuitable for them. On the other hand, boots were compulsory, even in the great heat of summer, and were very heavy for their weak ankles; even in the rainy season they might not be changed, neither could goloshes be worn. A day was fixed for the donning of white linen uniforms, and this had to be adhered to, even if the weather were abnormally cold. On occasions when the Emperor drove publicly through the streets the Peers' School lined the road, and were forbidden to wear any overcoats, no matter how cold a wind there might be, or how many hours they had to stand. Coats were also discarded at funerals, which, alas, my pupils were often obliged to attend, and serious chills were frequently contracted in consequence.

Funerals are associated with strict etiquette in Japan, and much importance is attached to them. Those inferior in position are usually expected to represent their family on such occasions. The husband, as a rule, does not attend the funeral of his wife; she, on the other hand, would go to her husband's funeral as chief mourner, dressed entirely in white. In our household the eldest Prince was represented at funerals by his gentlemen attendants, or in the case of an important personage, by his younger brothers. Should an Imperial Prince or a celebrity die, Prince Shimadzu used himself to attend in person.

There was no fixed gymnastic afternoon at the school; lessons were given between the classes, and jerseys were not worn, neither were braces discarded.

The boys took more readily to baseball than to cricket, I suppose because it was played in school. When the British ships came to Yokohama there were often cricket matches between the naval men and those in the diplomatic and consular service, but the Japanese never seemed very keen, although great interest was shown by the students in the baseball teams sent abroad.

The mid-day meal was quite a secondary consideration, and consisted of a little fish, rice and pickles in a luncheon-box, with chop-sticks for use. There was no one to supervise the meals, and a pupil would often leave his food half finished in order to get in more time for play.

The lessons themselves and the arrangement of the work was different from our own schools. The children were not allowed to prepare lessons for the coming day, by which means a competitive spirit would have been aroused among them; classes were formed according to height and regardless of merit, and the subjects taken were far too many for young minds to tackle. But little by little these difficulties were overcome. As the school was within walking distance, the boys were allowed to come home for an early dinner, and I set to work to supervise their preparation. A good home teacher was appointed, and special attention was paid to their writing, which is such an important study in Japanese eyes that charms are often obtained from their temples to ensure a child against writing badly.

On the whole, the little boys were decidedly happy in their school life, and the fact that detention from school was considered to be a form of punishment speaks well for the Gaksuhin.

At one time the school had a most earnest President, who did everything in his power for the boys' good, but from the beginning to the end I had a big fight to enforce my own views on the subject of their education. The Prince was in the middle class, which presented even greater difficulties than in the case of his small brothers. Many of the teachers seemed to be most lethargic both in discipline and in punctuality, and I sometimes wondered if they regarded their pupils as too great to exact obedience from them. The masters were often absent for days at a time, and the boys naturally took advantage of their freedom and followed their own devices instead of doing their work. The Prince and his friends occasionally made walking expeditions which lasted for two or three days, during which time they would put up at various tea-houses on the way! There was little or no proper supervision, and as my charges mixed freely with boys of all classes, the influences surrounding them were not always good, and I had many an anxious hour. But by degrees great changes and improvements were wrought, both in the middle class and in other parts of the school.

Japanese teachers as a class certainly hold a far more respected position than in England. A private teacher is not usually paid by arrangement, owing to the fact that custom avoids all monetary discussions, but the teacher is no loser by this, for the Japanese are exceptionally generous in matters of the kind. It is generally arranged that a present (which is certain to be a good one and to include money) is made by the pupil or by his parents, but it is given in a way which avoids any appearance of payment for the lessons received. The idea is that the honour of being entrusted with the child's education is a sufficient reward in itself, but whether the honour places the teacher in a more responsible position I do not know.

To add to my difficulties, and greatly to my surprise, I found that the children brought back messages from their teachers saying what was to be done at home in matters quite apart from their lessons, and as many of their ideas of education were utterly opposed to my own, this interference was most undesirable. On looking carefully into the matter, I found that most of the pupils at the Nobles' School were left entirely to the care of attendants, though doubtless they each had guardians; and that in many cases advice would be sorely needed in the matter of education. This seeming interference was, therefore, quite accounted for; but I was determined that the teachers should have no control in our home.

Among the masters were one or two whom I must acknowledge as helpers. I used to go up to the school and watch my charges at work in their classes, and I often found great sympathy from the teachers in my efforts towards their improvement. Some of them spoke English very well.

The teacher of the youngest boy gave me a weekly report, written in English, and I was much touched by receiving one on his term's work even after I had left Japan. The English of it may not be quite perfect, but if a similar report were made in Japanese by an Englishman he might well be proud. It was as follows:

"His energy is increasing by and by, and his studies are effective. The teachers of the Gaksuhin admire of his development. His future must be bright. I was once anxious of his study, now I am at ease. His attention is becoming intense more and more. His activity becoming more quick than ever. He studies every day as if Miss Howard were governing over him yet. All keeping past condition. He must be gratified of Miss Howard."

This shows great sincerity and earnestness on the teacher's part. He was most anxious to improve his pupil and to keep him up to the mark, and I have kept this report as a proof of my appreciation.

Once or twice a year a very solemn ceremony is held in the Gaksuhin, and, I believe, in all the schools. It is the passing in front of the Emperor's portrait, and it is regarded more or less as a religious ceremony. At ordinary times the portrait is hidden by curtains and is kept in a special room, but on the Emperor's birthday the President draws aside these curtains and the Imperial portrait is revealed to the teachers and pupils. Then, in solemn silence and with great respect, they pass before the portrait, teachers and pupils alike, making their bows. This intense and devoted loyalty is inherent in the Japanese nation, together with their deep reverence for the dead, which is indeed the outcome of their religion. It is considered disrespectful to look down from a window on the dead, and, in the same manner, no one must gaze on the Emperor from a higher place than he himself occupies. By the same rule, when the Emperor drives past the houses of the people all the windows of the houses must be closed, and everyone must stand in solemn silence. The students are not permitted to wear overcoats, and they must be attired in their best holiday clothes this in itself being almost a ceremonial act.

Students usually have a school uniform, which they are obliged to wear except in the holidays, when they go back to the comforts of a kimono. Both girl and boy students wear a divided skirt called a hakama, which is made of silk for best occasions, and of a material like serge for every- day use. The colour of these divided skirts differs according to the school; red is the most popular, the difference being marked chiefly by various shades, although blue is also a favourite. To the unaccustomed eye of the European these Japanese students appear exactly alike, it is almost impossible to tell one from the other. In matters of education Japan has taken a wonderful lead in the East; Tokio has many thousands of students from China, who dress in the same way as the people of the town, and numbers of Japanese girls leave their country every year to take situations as governesses in Siam and other Eastern places.

Many students show signs of overwork and late hours in the constant use they make of spectacles; the Japanese characters are, doubtless, very trying for close reading. They do not wear a pince-nez, but invariably a pair of gold-rimmed spectacles, such as one's grandparents used. Their zeal for learning English is somewhat trying to a foreigner at times. For example, I found it quite impossible when staying in Kamakura to sit quietly by the sea and read a book. A Japanese student would be sure to come and plant himself by my side with the idea of self-improvement. No matter how limited his English he would attempt a conversation; the less his command of the language, the more inquisitive he would appear to be. The following is a specimen of the conversation:

"You have got father? Where you live? What you do? Why you come to Japan?"

It was often very trying.

Japanese reading in private is a hard study, and has one noticeable peculiarity, that it is carried on aloud. I used to hear a continual intoning going on under my room, very loud and very monotonous. On inquiring the reason I discovered it was the attendants reading to themselves. In the office downstairs, while the attendants were adding up accounts, one heard a kind of chant going on, and wherever we went the same sounds were to be heard. A book is rarely read in silence, but in shops a silent reckoning is made, aided by an instrument called a soroban, similar to the kindergarten beads used for teaching arithmetic. In giving an estimate for anything at a shop this instrument never fails to make its appearance, and I never discovered why the sonorous sounds of counting were always to be heard in the office.

Besides the home-teacher, who was engaged for the preparation work, the Guardians appointed a well-known historian to come on Sunday evenings for six months and give lectures on the history of the Shimadzu family, so that the Prince and his brothers might learn more of their ancestors. The history of the family dates back over one thousand years, and it, therefore, needed many months of study. These lectures lasted an interminable time and the listeners generally returned worn out, and once I was asked to speak most seriously to one of the children who had fallen asleep during the discourse; it was regarded as a great honour for him to be present, as his smaller brothers were not admitted. The lectures started with an attendance of forty, all of whom were invited to tea afterwards, but, with due respect to the historian, I fancy they must have been deadly dull and uninteresting, for the ranks of listeners thinned each week, and the family showed an unmistakable dread when the date fixed for the next lecture drew near. I doubt whether their ancestors were more reverenced in consequence.

Story-telling has a great place in the life of Japan. In the streets one sometimes comes across a crowd of little children round a central figure, very often that of an old man, whose daily earnings consist of the cents thrown by these small listeners out of gratitude for the tales he has to relate tales of knighthood, and of the brave heroes of old, which stimulate the young to deeds of courage. It is also quite usual at entertainments for young people to engage a professional story-teller of this kind.

CHAPTER VII

IN spite of the pressure of work I managed to take a daily walk. The roads in Tokio were a great surprise to me, for with a few exceptions in one part of the town there were no pavements or side-walks for pedestrians. The roads had deep ditches each side, and no drainage like our gutters, consequently they were continually getting filled up with mud and dirt, and often had to be cleared out, a most unhealthy proceeding, which made the smells very objectionable, especially in summer. After rain had fallen in large quantities the mud in the roads became very thick, and, should a hot sun come to dry this up, deep ruts would be made in the road, which soon became positively painful to walk over. In hot weather water-carts appeared drawn by coolies, whose method of watering was somewhat entertaining. They would sometimes dash along at full speed, leaving dry patches, and at other times stop to take breath, leaving a patch on the road well deluged with water. It was also a common thing to see a householder come out with a pail of water and small ladle, to do his or her bit of watering outside the house.

Before I got accustomed to the streets of Japan I found walking quite a strain on my nerves. It impressed me as being most perilous, and the indifference to danger shown by the working men and boys, as they threaded their way through the crowds of pedestrians, handcarts and jinrickshas was extraordinary. Bicycles, too, simply flew along, and the riders were often weighted with heavy bundles on their backs, which stuck out most unpleasantly, especially in turning corners.

The jinrickshas were drawn at a terrifying speed, especially those of the doctors, which had red wheels to distinguish them from the other traffic, and it seemed to me incredible that there were not collisions and accidents every few moments. The kurumaya, or jinricksha men, are wonderful runners, and do not seem to find any inconvenience in the straw sandals which they are obliged by law to wear since plague was introduced through the rats. Most of them, at any rate in Tokio, wore dark blue cotton kimonos, and I never anywhere came across the unclothed multitude which hearsay had led me to expect. It was quite surprising to see the enormous weights that the coolies could carry, nothing seemed too much for them, and they pulled their little heavily-laden carts with such ease that one can quite understand how the Japanese are able to dispense with horses and use man-power instead.

The streets often have an appearance of fairyland—one suddenly encounters a tall tree in full bloom being taken to a new place to be replanted in fresh soil, an endless string of coolies drawing it along. Within a few days this tree will blossom as vigorously as ever.

On one of my first walks I passed a cart-load of Japanese pickles the smell of which nearly knocked me down. They are mostly made out of vegetables, such as radishes and turnips, and are preserved in salt and a mixture of rice. The Shimadzu children seemed to love these pickles and quite ignored their smell, and if asked on the occasion of their birthdays to choose a favourite meal it would invariably be a Japanese one, with an extra share of pickles. As a retort to my disparaging remarks they would give ideas on the smell of cheese! On a birthday rice is coloured by a mixture of red beans, this being the only form of feasting in Japan to take the place of a birthday cake.

The street vendors, dragging their carts along, are a regiment in themselves. I can still hear, in my mind, the shrill whistle of the pipe-sellers, and see the ice-cream and " sweet " sellers, followed by crowds of joyful little children, with bright eyes and brilliant coloured kimonos, running along behind them on wooden clogs, which looked perilous for such tiny feet, especially when a small person had a fat baby tied to his or her back. How they managed not to fall was a wonder.

The contrast between European riding and that of the Japanese was very noticeable; the horse's pace was a marvel in itself, and both rider and beast might have been dozing. A betto or coolie invariably ran by the side of the horse with a paper broom in his hand to flick off the flies and whip the sleeper into action. It struck me as a poor display, and made the surprise all the greater when later on the Cavalry regiments so distinguished themselves in the war.

Mr. Nagasaki kindly arranged Sunday drives, and in spite of his very busy life would frequently accompany us, which enabled us all to understand one another better. The obedience, patience, contentment and stoicism of my charges, even down to the youngest child, impressed me greatly. I remember one day when we drove for many hours and Yonosuke was overcome with sleep in the carriage. His brothers aroused him, and he accepted this as a reproof. It was wonderful to see so young a boy battling against fatigue and sleep.

We went to many exhibitions, one of the most interesting being pictures painted on silk. This kind of painting is very disheartening. An artist will often half finish his picture before discovering a flaw in the silk, which obliges him to start afresh, as these flaws make it impossible to paint the picture. The subjects chosen by Japanese artists struck me as being very poetical.

Apart from the paintings, the exhibitions impressed me as being so different from ours with our heavy gold frames. Japanese pictures are all hung on wooden scrolls. The tortoise and crane are depicted everywhere, representing long life and happiness, and the Four Seasons is also a favourite source of inspiration. I remember one Japanese picture of a goddess (or Madonna as the interpreter called her) represented as the mother of eight dragons, which are the eight passions. She was not beautiful. Also I recall a strange picture of a group of tiny naked children, with a central figure wearing a halo round his head, which apparently represented Christ. The artist told me the following story about it. " These children live in a country, it is neither heaven nor hell. They have died, and are picking up stones, trying to build castles; as they pick them up they count them, saying, 6 one for mother, one for father,' etc. These are supposed to be the children's prayers. There is a wicked spirit round them trying to pull down, as the little ones build, but the central figure is by their side, though unseen by the children, and His presence will enable them to complete the building."

We were shown two wonderful vases, which had taken eighteen people five years to make. The names of all the workers were engraved on the bottom of the vases, which were of gold and silver.

The Japanese have discovered a marvellous method of mixing metals which produces delightful shades and colours, and is used for representing landscapes. We were shown several beautiful boxes and vases made from this curious compound, and many other treasures which have not as yet reached the Western world.

When we went on these expeditions, I noticed that the Prince carried a note-book, in which he would enter any fresh English word that occurred in course of conversation; and that he was also armed with a Japanese dictionary. He was extraordinarily earnest for his age, in fact, my pupils all were, and would generally prefer to look at illustrated papers or books of photographs, rather than to play games, if given a choice of entertainment. They all were much less active than Western boys, which, however, was solely due to their being sons of Japanese nobility.

At that time I was subjected to a great deal of staring whenever the Prince, his brothers, and the gentlemen were with me. On Sundays Mr. Nagasaki used to take us to see the temples and other sights of Tokio, and the crowds on these occasions were very trying.

When visiting the temples a Shinto priest was often sent to meet us, who generally presented paper handkerchiefs to the Prince and his party for drying their hands, which they were expected always to wash in a tank of water usually placed outside the temple. In going up to the shrine each worshipper made a bow, but the gentlemen attendants often clapped their hands as well as bowing, which (the children told me) they did in order to get the attention of the gods. Hence a clapping audience among foreigners must be somewhat mystifying to the Japanese mind.

At the shrine itself food was always to be found. Either a plate of oranges or dried fish and small vases of water were placed there, according to the Shinto custom of feeding the spirits.

Once, after a visit to one of the temples, the youngest boy, prompted by a sudden feeling of affection for me, solemnly promised, in saying good-night, that I should always have plenty of fish and food to eat at my shrine, as he would never forget me!

The visits to various flower gardens were a delight. The Japanese irises were most wonderful, and of so many different colours. Many of these are produced by means of cochineal, which is poured on to the roots of the growing flowers cut blossoms are sometimes dipped into it. But Japanese flowers, though so entrancing, have one thing lacking you do not find in them the sweet smell of our own dear, old-fashioned flowers, and this is certainly a disappointment. People told me that it was due to the torrents of rain during the rainy season, and if this is so it may also account for their vegetables having less flavour than our own.

Flowers seem almost like human things to the Japanese, and the frequent shows are most popular events in their districts, large crowds wending their way to the show places as the seasons come round. No doubt the pride of the people centres in the cherry tree, with its amazing wealth of blossom, but the plum has also its share of appreciation. The fruit of neither is particularly good, as everything is sacrificed to the flowers, and all cultivation tends towards the production of the wonderful blossoms for which the country is famous. The chrysanthemum, which is associated with so many things in Japanese life, and is also used as the Imperial crest, is, perhaps, the favourite of all the other flowers, but the azalea and the iris are greatly prized by the throngs of visitors to the shows.

Many trees and flowers represent virtues to the Japanese mind. For instance, the bamboo is thought to be a type of gentleness, and the hardy little plum tree, which is brave enough to blossom even when the snow has fallen, is said to resemble a sorrowing soul which still keeps a steadfast faith. It is as if each tree and flower voiced a message. There is, indeed, an indescribable difference between our flower shows and those of the Japanese.

One particularly interesting visit was to the Imperial Gardens, and as these gardens were never opened to the public I was greatly envied by some of the foreigners. There were a great number of tea-houses, where the Emperor used to take tea, and as we came to each of these, Mr. Nagasaki stopped and raised his hat, the Princes and the rest all following his example. We were shown a famous painting on silk of a large falcon, which will always be of historical interest in Japan. It flew on board a man-of-war at the time of the war between China and Japan, and was welcomed as a messenger of coming victory, which it proved to be.

Animals were kept in these gardens, among them a monkey, storks, two kangaroos and quantities of birds. These little birds were in small wooden cages, beautifully made and all alike; they were placed closely together, on a stand, like flower-pots in a conservatory. The poor mites were beating their little wings against the sides of these cramped cages. Their palatial life certainly seemed a very fettered one. There was, however, one exception in a bird whose cage was large enough to enable it to fly round in circles. I am reminded of a Japanese custom at a funeral, which it may be of interest to note. On the way to the grave a cage of birds is sometimes seen in the procession. This cage is kept untouched until after the burial, when the birds are allowed to fly away a charming allegory which signifies the soul's escape, fettered no longer by mortal things. It has since struck me that one never sees nor hears of boys going birds'-nesting in Japan, and I think that this custom may partly explain why they refrain from doing so.

CHAPTER VIII

THERE is no whole holiday in Japan during the year when all shops are closed; the nearest approach to a general holiday is New Year's Day, and due advantage is taken of the endless temple feast-days and of Sundays, when the streets are crowded with holiday makers. The merry, good-natured looks on the faces of the people, the universal love they showed for their children, and the way in which the aged always accompanied the family on their outings and were tenderly guarded, was quite touching. On our excursions my eyes were involuntarily riveted on the pink, blue or white knitted European shawls, which the women of the middle class invariably wore over their shoulders. They seemed entirely to spoil the pretty effect of the kimonos and the artistic national dress.

The horses all appeared more or less like ponies, so much smaller were they than our own; the dogs in the road also struck me as looking very different and not half so attractive. But there was pleasure to be found in the cocks and hens, which strutted all over the place, and even in the roads. They had a familiar touch of home about them.

We went to the Zoological Gardens, the grounds of which are far prettier than our own. The best traditions of the Japanese garden are to be found there, furnished as it is with little bridges, steps and ponds. The roofs of the animals' cages are very decorative, but I don't think the inmates have as good a time as our animals, owing to lack of room in which to dispose themselves.

One of our expeditions was to the Prince's large Japanese house, a very long drive away. It was my first introduction to his sisters, of whom he had a great many, though all were married before I was appointed, except three, who lived in this most beautiful home. My first visit was a painful ordeal; the whole place was crowded with attendants, both ladies and gentlemen. There were two sentinels outside the entrance gate, and the drive up to the house seemed endless. On the left was a green bank, and behind this, half hidden, were many bowing people. These were the retainers, who still adhered to the old custom of regarding the Prince as too great to be met face to face. The rows of attendants' houses were also partly hidden by this bank for the same reason.

On arriving we found the front door already opened, and a large number of gentlemen thronging the entrance. Behind, in an inner hall, stood the three sisters and a few ladies. One of the Princesses was grown up and was dressed in European style, one was a schoolgirl of about fifteen years, and the third was a beautiful little girl of about five years of age, who burst out crying, as if in terror, at seeing a European face.

My first surprise at the meeting between the brothers and sisters was to see the obeisances with which the sisters met their eldest brother. It was a silent exchange of bows, of a most reverent and formal kind. We were taken down long passages to a room with European carpet, chairs and table. Otherwise the house was completely Japanese and perfectly beautiful. We were all placed round the table, the one and only arm-chair being graciously given to me. It was very embarrassing; if I rose from my chair on being asked to look at something, everyone else rose too.

Some of the old gold lacquer was extraordinarily fine, and there was a beautiful hibachi, or square stove, which is used for heating purposes, and can be carried about and placed by the side of any particular person or persons. After a time we were taken into a room especially set apart for the tea ceremony. It seemed to hold fewer things, if possible, than the ordinary Japanese room. But there was the same softly padded floor of tatami, the alcove and its representative altar with the hanging kakemono, the age and beauty of which were quite unsurpassable, and there was a most delightful hanging pot, containing a very few flowers arranged with thoughtful care. The hibachi was made of solid silver. On it was placed a cauldron, made of gold which had been brought from the Prince's mine. A smell of incense, from wafers placed on the red ashes, was perceptible. Such a stove and kettle could only be used on a highly ceremonious occasion.

The art of tea making is quite a study and a necessary part of education for the daughters of the nobility. Each movement has been gracefully acquired, from the dusting and washing of the cups and basin to the walking on the padded floor. The tea-maker's small feet are covered with spotlessly white socks or tabbis. The cultivation of this art (for it is an art) produce beautiful carriage and manners in a woman. Certainly there is something representative of the Japanese ideal of woman in this ceremony. Here she reigns supreme, serving others in the home and dispensing hospitality in silence and reserve. Some speak of tea making as a religious ceremony, and compare the room dedicated for the purpose to a chapel attached to one of our big houses. It did not strike me as such. But I felt its influence during the solemn silence.

The preparation was lengthy, as there were so many preliminaries to be gone through. When the water appeared to have reached boiling point, the first duty was to cool it off. The Princess took a ladle, which lay on a stand by her side, and ladled out some cold water, which she poured into the kettle. She then measured out two and a half teaspoons full of green powdered tea, placed them in a wonderful silver bowl and added one and a half ladles of water from the kettle. This she stirred with a bamboo whisk (rather like an egg-beater), with the result that the tea became frothy. With superb courtesy and grace the little hostess handed me the drink. Etiquette requires that the guest should drink it in three gulps, and short sentences are spoken between the tea-maker and her guest, but I was not initiated into these words or their meaning. I managed to drink off the full contents of the cup, but must confess that the aftereffects of insomnia lasted two or three nights. The experience, however, was worth any amount of wakefulness. It left a calmness and gave a sense of peace not easily forgotten. As a memento of this interesting ceremony the Princess presented me with a fan.

The old Japanese gardens are as like fairyland as can be. After the tea ceremony we wandered round the garden, but it was too cold for sitting in the various tea-houses, which are used in summer for enjoying the different views the garden offers. I noticed a little iron house painted black, somewhat resembling a temple, which was spoken of as the " Go-down." Later on, I found that this was a large storehouse, where the most valuable treasures are kept, to be guarded against fire or the breakage which a great earthquake might entail.

On returning to the house we were taken to a large room where the Prince's little sister had just kept her annual dolls' festival. Innumerable dolls were placed on long wooden shelves against the wall. These shelves were covered with red material and were in tiers, recalling the inside of a miniature theatre. A great many of the dolls were family heirlooms and were hundreds of years old. They are only brought out of the go- down once a year, for three days, being far too precious to see daylight except on a festive occasion. March 3rd is kept as an especial feast day for little girls, and fortunately we had arrived in time to see the dolls all arranged. In the centre were the doll images, representing the Emperor and Empress of the past, and along each side were dolls dressed in the oldest Japanese fashions of centuries back. They seemed to be arranged more or less according to their rank, dolls of lesser importance being seated on the lower shelf. Besides these dolls there were beautiful lacquer bowls and sake cups, filled with minute portions of food and wine. On the lowest shelf were all things appertaining to a lady's toilet, such as combs and rouge for the lips; also a small kind of razor for shaving the eyebrows and some stuff for blackening the teeth, both of which were ordered to be used by the widows of old. It was indeed an interesting collection, and the little Princess gazed upon it with a look of joy and pride, in great contrast to the tear-stained little face that met us at the entrance.

When a girl marries she takes her innumerable doll family to her new home, and still keeps the feast until the arrival of a small daughter enables her to hand the dolls over to a younger generation. Motherhood-love is early implanted in the heart of the little Japanese girl, and her doll is an important factor in life. It is invariably beside her, but she plays with and enjoys it in a manner different from that of her little English sisters. Her doll is strapped on to her back, inside her kimono, in the same way as her own baby brothers and sisters are carried. She cannot handle it or play with it, but she is proudly and happily conscious of its presence. You can see her running about and playing games, with her treasure always tucked into her kimono. It is a charming picture, this tiny Japanese mother flitting about in her kimono of many soft colours.

There is, also, another occasion on which a doll is taken away by its owner. If a little child dies it is customary to place a doll in the coffin, by way of companionship to the little one when passing through the valley of death. There are many extraordinary customs in this ancient country of Japan, and behind them all some loving and touching meaning is always to be found.

Separate names also appear to be given by the Buddhist priests to individuals, by which they are addressed after death. Priests are employed, so I was told, to pray for the dead, and payment is made for these intercessions according to the length of the prayers.

Some of the names of Japanese girls are very characteristic of the nation. Lovers of nature, they name their daughters after her most beautiful objects, such as Snow or Sunshine. Boys' names, however, are of a sterner kind. The names of wild animals, such as Tiger or Bear, and objects of strength, such as " Stones," are chosen.

The distinctive " ichi-ban " often met with in Japanese is almost identical with our expression of AI in English, except that it carries with it a far higher sense of approbation. Ichiban literally means " Number One." In its full significance it refers to the first-born son of the family, and it is, therefore, symbolical of all that is held precious and sacred. It is the standard of perfection. In conversation it expresses the highest approval. In Japan, ichiban means man, for the weaker vessels women have as yet scarcely reached to so high a standard as Number One in any walk of life! On leaving the Prince's house we carried back cakes with us, an invariable custom among the Japanese. Wherever one goes, even after an audience of the Empress or Princesses, one is given cake, tasting somewhat like sponge cake, which is cut into square blocks and wrapped in a kind of butter muslin. A few days after visiting the Prince's sisters I paid my first call, and had tea with a Japanese family. The cake was terribly indigestible and made of cocoanut and sugar, with a hard green outside, like the bark of a tree and just like wood to bite. I was told to be sure and eat the outside, and politeness obliged me to do so, but I suffered!

I am reminded of the great joy which was shown about this time, in the month of May, at the birth of the present Crown Prince. When six days old he was carried to the Emperor's Palace, where a small scroll was unrolled in the presence of all the courtiers, and his name, which until then had been kept a profound secret, was read out. The name given to him was: Michi-no Miya hiro hito.

On this occasion one hundred and one guns were fired, and fireworks were let off all day long.

The result of all this sight- seeing was a growing desire on the part of the Prince and his brothers to take photographs. Cameras were, therefore, bought. The story of the first photograph, taken by one of the youngest children, is so quaint and also such an example of the contrast between the old and young generations of Japan, that I am tempted to relate it in full. The photograph of an attendant standing with his hat on was expected by the young photographer, but on developing it the attendant appeared both hatless and headless. The child came to me in a fury of indignation that an attendant should show such disrespect as to allow himself to be photographed without a head, in spite of the fact that the shadow of the figure had come out with both head and hat. As I tried to appease him, and to plead pardon for the poor innocent attendant, the Daimyo of old flashed across my mind. He it was, who, when enraged with a vassal, would frequently give an order of " off with his head." Times certainly are changed I thought.

The Princes' sisters had a retinue of lady attendants, and one or two of these invariably accompanied them on occasions when they came to visit us in the European house; otherwise, I had very little intercourse with them. They showed untold devotion to each member of the family, and it was very evident that it pained them for the brothers to be so entirely separated from their sisters. Some of these ladies were of a great age, but astonishingly active and hearty. One, in particular, was to be admired. She was most sporting in undertaking long walks and accompanying the Princesses, and no matter how long an entertainment might be she sat steadily through it.

Some of them seemed to have especial duties allotted to them. One was exclusively employed in attending to the ancestral shrine all Shinto worshippers possess a shrine in their house. She had to supply the food offerings, and to clap her hands and bow her head in worship.

I used to find in the children's cupboards in their bedrooms pieces of wood with letters on them and a stamp of the temple, which they told me she had given them. They appeared to be amulets, which, according to Shinto belief, are necessary safeguards against dangers and sorrows. Some children are weighed down by these amulets. A friend of mine found them sewn up in a child's frock; in this case they were like small pieces of lead. A priest often gives cake to the worshippers at the temples, and I frequently found small cakes stowed away in the cupboards sent from the same source. It seemed to me that these lady attendants were all full of superstitious practices, but they never interfered with me and were most retiring, taking a very humble position with the Prince and his brothers. If they were given any little gift by the latter their gratitude was untold. Once, when the children brought back several bottles of eaude-Cologne from their travels, they sent them to these little ladies. The result was a telephone message a few days later, asking how much of this eau-de-Cologne was usually drunk, as they found it had affected their heads. They had believed it to be European wine!

Some time after my arrival we went for the day to Kamakura, about two hours' journey by train, to visit some of the ancestral shrines. We ascended a flight of steps, and found the first sacred spot at the top of a steep hill. The surrounding scenery was remarkably fine, but quite the most attractive spot was to be found in the grounds of the famous Diabutsu or Great Buddha, which we afterwards visited. Among the Buddhas in Japan none can compare with this figure. The deity itself represents Amida. Some people say this Buddha was brought from China, others that it was made in Korea and brought over in pieces to be erected on the site where it now stands. The image is in bronze and of very large dimensions, the thumb alone measuring three feet in circumference. A ladder leads up to the head, and the interior of the figure is a shrine.

Kamakura has twice been visited by tidal waves which swept away the adjacent temple building, leaving there, in majestic solitude, the sacred figure calm and quite untouched, except where time had beautified the colouring.

I saw all around me the signs of winter and change and, as I stood looking, the image seemed to prove the eternity of goodness. At a later date when we were staying in Kamakura I used often to sit there by the hour, and the wonderful, calm, dignified and grand expression on the face always put peace into my heart. The Buddha, in the midst of such lovely scenery, was as a calm centre the essence of all good.

CHAPTER IX

A GENTLEMAN informed me in the early spring of 1901 that we were to have a two months' trip, visiting Kobe, Kyoto and other places. We started at the end of one month and returned, much to my surprise, in the middle of the next. This was no false statement on the attendant's part; it only illustrated the difference in reckoning months. He merely meant that we should be away during certain days in two different months, and accordingly reckoned it as a period of that duration.

On this occasion I accompanied Prince Shimadzu on a ten days' trip, leaving his little brothers behind. It was our first experience in travelling together. I was advised not to take my amah for myself, and told that only one gentleman would go with the Prince.

The time chosen for the start by rail was an exceptionally early one, and necessitated our being at the station soon after 5 a.m., but this early hour did not lessen the number of attendants who were present to see the Prince off.

The language still proved a difficulty, as I had only been two months with the family, and, unfortunately, Mr. Yamasaki, who accompanied us, was unable to speak a word of English. I was very glad when at last the train steamed out of the station, leaving behind the many who had come to pay their respects.

It was very strange to see the ladies and gentlemen in a railway carriage taking off their clogs, putting them neatly together under the seat, and then sitting on their legs and feet. How they can sit in this position for more than a few minutes is a puzzle, but so they would remain for hours at a time quite comfortably.

Strange as it appeared to me at first, the women, when travelling, would produce a little case, and drawing from it a diminutive pipe would insert tobacco, light it, and then carefully empty out the bowl after but one puff, which appeared more a ceremony than an indulgence.

When travelling by railway the Japanese spend their time chiefly in eating. Luncheon boxes are always easily procured, and also a tea-pot and cup. These luncheon boxes are very neatly contrived, and they are made in three divisions. One place is especially reserved for rice, and the other two for pickles and fish respectively. They also contain a new pair of wooden chop-sticks. The price is surprisingly low, for the whole costs only a few pence.

For those who are accustomed to Japanese food and who can appreciate it these boxes are very nice and convenient, but, like other strange tastes, it is one which has to be acquired. The tea-pot, too, however desirable of its kind, is a source of grave disappointment to an ordinary European. Even if one could " understand " the tea, no milk nor sugar are obtainable.

Japanese travellers consume a great deal of fruit during a journey, and the eating of this often makes the carriages very undesirable, not to say stuffy.

A Japanese man does not exhibit the virtue of unselfishness when travelling. On the contrary, very much the reverse. He appears to think that he has the right to monopolize several seats in the carriage. He may make himself comfortable and lie down, indulging in far too deep a sleep to be easily aroused. Several of the seats will be filled with his belongings, and when other passengers come in and wish to occupy the places he seems to be riveted to the spot and unable to rouse himself.

Reaching Nagoya at four o'clock we went by jinrickshas to the hotel, and were received with a great deal of bowing and kowtowing.

Such a reception is not confined only to Princes and celebrities, but is extended to all visitors in Japanese hotels, both on arrival and departure. Not only do the many boys and amahs come and make their bows, but the proprietor and his several office clerks also generally manage to appear and to find some means of offering polite attentions. Naturally, however, these receptions were on a larger scale whenever Prince Shimadzu and his brothers went on a journey.

As this was our first travelling experience this visit was to be of a purely private nature, with the sole object of sight-seeing. No sooner had we finished tea than we started off in jinrickshas to see the old castle of Nagoya. The castle was surrounded by moats and high walls some eighteen feet thick, but of its general appearance I remember little beyond a mysterious scintillation that much puzzled me as we approached, and which seemed to appear now here, now there, as we changed our direction on the winding road. On arrival this proved to emanate from two magnificent golden dolphins, some eight feet high, presented in the seventeenth century by a very celebrated general, and valued at 36,000. One of these dolphins, when sent to an exhibition in Vienna, suffered shipwreck on its return journey, and was recovered at great trouble and expense.

My first morning without an amah and with no English-speaking maid was an amusing experience. Having rung for hot water and a cup of tea my difficulties began, and resulted eventually in a flat hip-bath being brought in, with a can of hot water and a plate with two pieces of toast, which was placed in the bath, and no tea!

Amongst other strange things to get used to, by the way, is the Japanese bath towel. It is made of a thin piece of cotton material, and usually has blue flowers printed on it. It is certainly not made for drying oneself after a bath being absolutely useless for that purpose. But it has its own function. When the towel is well saturated with water a Japanese bather wrings it out and uses it afresh. By the time that this method has been applied several times the body is comfortably moist, and there is no fear of being too quickly dried. Of course, it is a matter of taste.

We left early the next morning for Kyoto, a journey of eleven hours, and went straight to the Yaami Hotel, where the manager proved himself to be quite proficient in English, and frequently acted as interpreter. The hotel is built on a hill, commanding a fine view.

Immediately after tea we made our usual visits to temples, and then went over the electricity works, which drew their power from the rapids, and are included in the programme of all sightseers.

At the bottom of the hill, opposite our hotel, was a famous cherry tree, called a " night cherry," since it was seen at its best at night-time, and the cherry blossom fetes were in full swing. Not only there, but in all large cities, night festivals are periodically held near the temples. Long rows of booths are put up by vendors of all sorts of wares, and are gaily lit up by illuminated torches and glaring flames, revealing the most alluring trinkets, fancy ornaments and endless toys. Here the little singing-insect in its diminutive cage of fine bamboo and goldfish innumerable can be bought.

The stalls of tempting cakes, sweets and peanuts do a brisk trade, and many cents are flung away on visits to shows, very much in the same style as at our own fairs.

Some stalls sold plants and flowers of every description, including dwarf trees of all shapes, which added to the charm of the scenery. The wonderful old cherry tree was lit up by lanterns. Hundreds of people were sitting tea drinking, many more were running about, laughing and shouting and full of joy. Drums to attract visitors were incessantly beaten by the doorkeepers of the various shows. After a long day's outing, to return late at night to the hotel and find this fairy scene was indeed refreshing.

We made an excursion by train from Kyoto to Kameoka, about three quarters of an hour's run. It was a wonderful journey, the line having been cleverly cut through mountains, and we passed through no less than eight tunnels, between which the train ran in the open by the banks of a dashing river. On arrival, within a few minutes' walk we reached Hozu, and took a flat-bottomed boat to Arashiyama to go down the rapids. We found six chairs placed in this boat, and three coolies for punting it down the rushing water. It seemed horribly dangerous; the sensation was like that of being on a continual switch-back, and we got well splashed; but it was wonderful, especially at the turning points, to see how they avoided various rocks and the long boats of wooden rafts tied together which passed us. Eventually we found ourselves at Lake Biwa, a huge lake with mountains all round, and the very loveliest spot on earth. There is a grand old tree there, hundreds of years old, and bent into a most picturesque shape.

On our return we went along the canal by boat, passing almost entirely through tunnels, a long, cold, dark journey. The boat we were in was like a rabbit-hutch. How we all crept into it I don't know! They had carpeted the floor for us to sit on, and it was pitch dark inside, though outside we had lanterns hung to avoid colliding with other boats which passed us. To go slowly underground through a long tunnel, which seemed endless, was an awful change after sunning ourselves at that beautiful lake, and struck me as being rather typical of life. One day in perfect joy and happiness, another in abject misery but there was light at the end. As we went along I kept my eyes on a tiny white hole which gradually grew, and the light shone brighter and brighter.

We spent the next day at Nara, the Governor having kindly sent his carriage to meet us. The betto, who ran as footman, distinguished himself by rolling under the horses' legs. I thought he was done for, and it was not easy under the circumstances to sit still; however, he seemed to pull himself together. The crowd was terrible. The Governor afterwards expressed his regret that we should be subjected to such pressure, but said it was an entirely new idea for the Prince to be seen driving with a European lady.

Nara was the capital of Japan over a thousand years ago, but time has greatly changed this once famous city, and from being a large, important town it has become quite a small place.

We were given luncheon at the club, which was a lovely Japanese house. The Governor and members were most kind and considerate in suggesting that I should keep on my boots, which seemed quite an impossibility when I looked at the spotless floor of the tatami. The hotel manager unknown to me had brought European food with him, but hearing that a Japanese luncheon had been prepared for us in a room alone I dispensed with the familiar viands, and gladly tasted my first real Japanese meal, using chop-sticks as an experiment. It was merciful that others were not present. Chop-sticks need practice, as I found to my cost and much to the Prince's amusement! It is quite easy to use them when once one has the knack, and later on I became quite proficient in handling them.

Cups of all sorts of soup and basins of fish, chicken, and endless unknown relishes came streaming in, and it seemed as if the meal would never be finished, but it was all so pretty to the eye and some dishes so pleasing to the taste that we felt in no hurry.

After luncheon we sat on a balcony overlooking a beautiful park with the tame deer running round eager to be fed. The horns of these animals are cut once a year for the safety of the public. The Governor took us over the club, where there was a large hall for Japanese dancing.

One impression still lingers in my mind of a visit we made to a Shinto temple in Nara, where a sacred dance was given for the Prince. I well remember the priest, robed in mauve satin, and the three Japanese girls with their powdered faces, each holding a fan dancing and kneeling to the accompaniment of three men, who sat on the floor with instruments which gave out a most wailing and dolorous sound. There sat the young Prince, and a sudden melancholy spirit seemed to possess us. At least, it thus affected me. There was something so piteously sad about it. What did it mean to them all I wondered. The manager informed me in a whisper that it was a prayer, and I recalled the little country church at home with its villagers and joyous choir, and I mentally compared this melancholy form of religion with our own, and longed to go back. The scene left its impression.

Our last day was spent in Kobe, and was the most enjoyable day of all.

We visited the Diabutsu or image of Buddha, which is quite different from the figure in Kamakura. It is far larger and over fifty feet in height, but is not so attractive looking, in fact rather the reverse, and no one could compare it with the beautiful Buddha of Kamakura. There was a very old copper temple bell to be seen, more than double the height of a man and very thick.

We also saw a unique sight in the trunk of a tree which actually produced from its one trunk seven other trees. I cannot remember their names, with the exception of the cherry and wisteria. It is one of the sights shown to all visitors.

One of Marquis Matsukata's sons met us, and most kindly took the Prince and myself over the large ship-building works there. Our visit to Mr. Matsukata's family was most enjoyable, as we received the kindest welcome from his wife, and also saw their beautiful little children. It brought back home to me and was a happy ending to our first visit away from Tokio.

CHAPTER X

ONE summer we were caught in the floods on our way up to Nikko. The train had not passed over the bridge half an hour before it fell down, and we found we could no longer reach the station. Jinrickshas, however, were procurable, and we had a five miles' run to the hotel. Every moment the floods grew worse, and finally we came to an impassable place where the situation became decidedly alarming. Two of the children were placed on the backs of coolies, who waded across, but the 'rickshas and the rest of the party had to ascend a high hill to get round to the other side of the river, none of which was easily done. On this occasion, three persons were drowned right in front of the hotel, and several people lost their lives. It was then that the celebrated and beautiful old red lacquered bridge, which only the Emperor might cross, was destroyed. A new one now takes its place, and doubtless in generations to come will be as greatly venerated, but very many hundreds of years must pass before it becomes as beautiful in colouring as the old one. In the hotel we heard a constant noise like thunder going on all day, caused by the huge boulders falling from the mountains into the rushing water below. It was a depressing and saddening sound.

There are generally about two typhoons a year. The most distinct in my mind is that which often arrives in September, but which has appeared as early as August. It is generally a break-up of summer, and is quite a regular visitor. The worst typhoon I experienced in Tokio was when, looking out of the window, I saw the brick wall in the garden partly blown down, and a tree torn up by the roots as easily as a weed might be. Once, when we were staying in Miyanoshita, a typhoon was raging for three days, and we were quite unable to move out of the house. Bridges were broken, and the whole place flooded. We had to walk on two wooden planks to reach the dining-room. A family staying in the hotel were booked to leave for Australia on the boat, but were prevented from doing so owing to the trains not running.

The tidal wave is doubtless one of the most awful visitations in Japan. Years ago the town of Kamakura, where the Prince has his country house, was entirely destroyed by a flood, and often at nights I used to lie and wonder if it might not happen again. During my sojourn a tidal wave came to Odawara, a place not far from there. It is awful beyond words when it comes, burying hundreds in its waves.

Our visit to Nikko is a pleasant remembrance, in spite of the rain which fell incessantly the whole time we were there. The scenery is fine, and various kinds of beautiful coloured mosses are to be seen.

Another visit which I enjoyed was to Ashinoya, on the way to Lake Hakone. We made the ascent from Yumoto in Chinese chairs, each having four bearers. It was a terribly steep ascent, and we broke the journey half way, stopping at a tea-house. On arriving at Ashinoya we found Mr. Nagasaki and his family, who had kindly prepared for us. This was my first experience of visiting sulphur springs, with their well-known suggestion of rotten eggs; to drink the water was most objectionable at first, but in time one got quite accustomed to it.

After a few days we went to Hakone Hotel, which we reached just in time to see the sunset and the great Fuji Mountain reflected on the lake an unforgettable moment.

At the time of our arrival the hotel was overrun by rats, and as Japanese beds are on the floor I found it somewhat difficult to sleep, knowing the possibility of being attacked during the night. Soon afterwards I believe they were exterminated, so we were unfortunate in the date of our visit.

Our stay was quite a short one, but before leaving we visited the Palace, and were given an audience of the Emperor's two eldest daughters, aged fourteen and fifteen years.

The presentation was a somewhat trying ordeal, as Mr. Nagasaki was unable to accompany us, and there was no one who could speak English in the Palace. The Prince paid his visit first, during which time I waited in a small room; several of the courtiers, with the kindest intentions, came into the room, but we were unable to converse.

I had been given a pair of carpet slippers, a very thoughtful and kind attention, as the floors strike one as somewhat cold after discarding one's boots. Unfortunately, these slippers were exceptionally large and difficult to keep on, and when the call for my audience came I had a long passage to go down and endless attendants were watching me. On entering, I found a long table placed at the end of the room, at which the two Princesses were seated with their courtiers. There was not a sound in the room, and apparently all that was expected of me was to make my bows and depart. This I did, but my slippers proved faithless. In spite of all efforts, I left one behind!

The formality in the presence of these two Princesses was quite unnerving, and compared with the simplicity and ease of the European audiences granted to me appeared very trying.

The Prince once took me up to Gifu for one or two nights to see the cormorant fishing which is one of the sights of Japan, and is quite one of the oldest sports in the world. There is a river, called Nagara, near Gifu, which is renowned for this particular kind of fishing. It can be only done in the dark, and getting into the flat-bottomed punt was not too easy! The water was lit up, however, by the blaze of flames coming from the charcoal braziers, which are sufficiently luminous for the birds to be seen plainly. A fine sight they were, too, and as keen sportsmen as could be, knocking against each other in their excitement to catch the fish. The fishermen held them by chains attached to a piece of bamboo, which was laid on the bird's back and secured to it by means of a cord round its body. There was also a metal ring round each bird's neck, placed rather low down.

It was a wonderful feat. With so much scampering and excitement collisions seemed inevitable, especially as each man would be holding in about a dozen birds; but the expert fishermen handled the reins somewhat after the style of the fairy dancer at a circus, who manages the ribbons so deftly as she drives and dances on the backs of the horses.

During the sport a man stood up in a boat, making a loud clatter with a bamboo instrument which is supposed to encourage the birds. A cormorant having captured a large fish (too big to pass down the throat, by reason of the ring round his neck) is a ludicrous sight, and has the appearance of being hopelessly drunk, swimming about most helplessly with the huge fish sticking out of his beak. Directly the fisherman sees there has been a catch he pulls in that particular bird, lifts him into the boat, forces open his bill and draws out the fish. A hard task, for whilst engaged in doing this he has all the other birds to curb and keep from fouling each other.

A huge quantity of fish was caught that night, and we much enjoyed watching the sport. There seemed no idea of any cruelty the birds were as happy as the fishermen and the spectators, enjoying many a tit-bit in the shape of small fish, which they were able to swallow in spite of their ring-bound throats.

CHAPTER XI

IN the New Year of 1902 we all moved to the house in Kamakura to spend the holidays there, and I had my first experience of living in a Japanese house. Like most of the houses of the nobility it stood in its own grounds and had a large wooden entrance-gate. Outside the house ran a piazza, where all boots and foot-gear had to be taken off before entering. For this reason I found boots a great nuisance, and envied the quickness with which a Japanese slipped his foot out of his wooden clog. The thick white calico socks, called tabbis, which cover the foot up to the lower ankle, leaving the leg bare, are also much more suitable to this style of house, and look far cleaner for walking on the mats which line the floors, being of a thicker material and a greater protection than our woollen stockings. But here again women's customs differ, for a Japanese woman thinks nothing of showing her bare leg, but keeps her arms well covered by way of politeness.

The tatami, or mats laid down in all Japanese rooms, are made of closely-compressed straw and are about one and a half inches thick, with a covering of finely woven rush matting. This forms a delicious floor for walking, sitting or lying on. The size of each room is reckoned by the number of its mats. A room can be so small as to contain only two or three, but an ordinary room would require eight or ten mats. The rooms are divided by sliding doors, and often in summer these are removed and the two rooms turned into one; the windows likewise slide, and there were wooden shutters, with paper in place of glass, called shoji. It is perfectly fascinating to discover how smoothly these slide, and how easily both doors and windows can be removed, so that the house becomes entirely exposed to the air. Other shutters, called amado, are put up at night, or in a heavy rainstorm during the day, but these are of heavy wood and closely fitting, something like those used for shopwindows. They run along the piazza, and are kept in a cupboard outside. Until one gets used to the amado, the sensation of being shut up in a wooden box is most uncomfortable. It is worth while to watch a Japanese lady open and shut one of these sliding doors. Etiquette demands that this be included in the curriculum of their education, just as much as tea making and the various forms of salutation. The ceremonial of opening and closing doors is most elegant and pretty. No bells are to be found in a Japanese house. Should you require the service of your maid you are expected to clap your hands. One notices this particularly when calling upon a Japanese household. It is the duty of the footman to shout your arrival, or if you are using a jinricksha the runner will likewise raise his voice loud enough to wake the dead. You are never kept waiting a pair of hands will always be found ready to slide back the wooden doors, and someone is always waiting to bow you either into, or away from, the house. This noisy style of entering a stranger's or acquaintance's garden is slightly embarrassing to the foreigner.

Japanese houses, as a rule, have no distinct rooms set apart for bedroom use; but this was not the case with the Prince's house in Kamakura, and we had European beds and fixed rooms to sleep in. Later on in our travels we often had to depend on Japanese beds, and I found them most comfortable, consisting as they do of soft, thick mattresses, called futons, covered with silk. They are kept in a cupboard during the daytime, brought out at night, and laid on the tatami. Early in the morning the futons are carried away with magical celerity, put out of doors in the sun and air for a time, and then returned to the cupboards. A Japanese house is blessed with endless cupboards, the doors of which also slide and look like a paper wall. They are about three feet long and very deep, and have a wonderful capacity for holding everything and anything, which enables a room to be kept constantly tidy.

There is next to no furniture in their houses. In the principal room there is an alcove, fitted with a piece of wood, raised a few inches above the floor. On this a vase of flowers invariably stands, and a kakemono, or hanging scroll of silk, upon which there is a picture, hangs above it on the wall. These scrolls are often hundreds of years old, and of great value. A small writingtable, usually made of lacquered wood, only a few inches high and about a yard in length, is also provided, and the boxes which hold the paper, brushes, and ink for writing lie on this table and are often made of beautiful old golden lacquer. The paper is in a long roll, and the ink consists of a stick of Indian ink, which is used by being dipped into water and rubbed on a stone. There is always a beautiful little ornament near for holding water, sometimes made in the shape of a minute European tea-pot or to represent an animal, with a hole in its body for pouring out the water. The writer holds his brush almost perpendicularly, and scarcely appears to touch the paper, his touch is so light. This is an art to be studied quite as much as painting, and the profession of it doubtless accounts for the fact that all Japanese show such great talent in painting.

My first impressions of living in a Japanese house during the summer have never changed, and I shall always prefer them to our European dwellings, with their crowded and heavy furniture and immovable window-frames. But my first night in Kamakura was not a success, and was, in fact, a most undesirable and memorable experience.

Having seen all the young people safely to bed, I went to my own room, accompanied by Koma. There was a howling wind, as near a typhoon as could be. The amado, or wooden shutters, were all tightly closed. So strong was the wind that it was almost impossible to hear any conversation, so I just turned in and dismissed the amah. I remember nothing more except that I woke somewhat late in the morning to find myself surrounded by people, and someone kindly saying they hoped I was better. I thought I was in a dentist's chair dreaming, but soon clearly understood that I had been chloroformed. My sliding windows had been found open, and my sheets and pillows were covered with green candle-grease. Part of my jewellery had been taken, but a suspicious selection had been made, for the most valuable articles had been left behind. Here, truly, was a proof of the necessity for guarding " the foreign lady," who had ,o foolishly willed to have it otherwise, and had caused the sentinels at the entrance-gate to be dismissed. Although I was never able to discover the culprit I was pretty well convinced that theft was not at the bottom of it, and that the outrage was due either to love for the young masters, shown in ignorance, or was meant to be a test of " the foreign woman's " courage. All I know is that, though at the time I received a great fright and a serious chill, owing to the open window, I shall ever regard this occasion as a great blessing in disguise. I faced the matter, and decided that if I communicated this to other foreigners not only should I cause a scare, but my work must necessarily cease. I determined, therefore, to place myself entirely in the hands of the Prince and his guardians, and reaped my reward, firstly in a most generous gift of jewellery, afterwards in untold protection all through my years of work; but above all, in winning the respect and trust of the attendants, who now ceased to regard my influence as weakening. Consequently, I never regretted this experience.

My first amah) Koma, did not remain with me for long; she was a wicked and dishonest little person, and fortunately I never met her like again during the whole of the remaining years I lived in Japan. She showed her vindictiveness at being dismissed by managing to boycott me for a short time, and thus preventing any other amah coming to me; but the name of the Prince's house soon overruled that difficulty, and the exchange was indeed a blessing to me.

Koma was a type of the Japanese one meets with in the Colonies. When afterwards, on visiting Canada and other places, I discovered that Japanese were to be had, I hastened to secure their services, but my experiences were often terrible, for the women I engaged were quite worthless characters. I don't think the Japanese are unique in this, for one often blushes for one's countrymen out in the Far East and the Colonies. Many who cannot get on at home take wing and fly far away, a proceeding which is greatly to be deplored for the sake of their country's reputation. Many a battle have I fought for the Japanese abroad, in trying to convince people that the type met with in the Colonies is not in the least characteristic of their countrymen at home.

As for one's own people, they have often grated on me in Japan. Once, when travelling with the children in a railway carriage which had not been reserved for them, a lady in the same compartment objected quite loudly to our coming in as we were too large a party, adding she did not want a lot of little monkeys in her carriage; all of which was clearly understood by my charges. I used to hear that these Europeans remind the Japanese of the native monkeys with red faces, which might have surprised me more had I not had somewhat the same experiences.

After having lived entirely among the Japanese for some months I went down one day to the sea-front at Kamakura, where I met some foreigners who were bathing in cotton kimonos. The extraordinary blueness of their eyes and their huge features and red faces made me for the moment think of the red monkeys!

The lack of tact and courteous consideration on the part of many English and Americans often pained and embarrassed me considerably, and especially the discourteous reference to Japanese of all classes as the " Japs," which is not only rude and lacking in respect, but is much resented by the people themselves. I have come across tourists who either through ignorance or want of ordinary common sense and feeling have made me thoroughly ashamed and furious.

I recollect once meeting a lady well-known in Western society who was travelling in Japan. She was of a very buoyant and high-spirited disposition, and of the ultra modern school of young women, not uncommonly met with abroad, who pride themselves upon their almost wild disregard of the usages of society when away from home. It was the occasion of an important official dinner, and she took out of a little silk bag a small, grey-looking powderpuff, and, addressing the man next to her in a clear voice, audible to everyone in the room, she said:

"Do you see that? This puff has powdered eight men's faces, and it shall now powder the ninth! v Whereupon she proceeded calmly to dab it at the face of her unfortunate dinner companion.

It is easy to imagine the thoughts of the highly sensitive Japanese who were present!

Another time I encountered a very, very upto-date lady tourist was on the occasion of a religious ceremony which was being held at night. It was extremely solemn and it was ordained that priests should jump over the flames of fire which were burning. I do not know its significance, but it was sufficient to see it was a sacred ceremony. This courageous young woman, suddenly, and to the utter consternation of the various diplomats and others standing round, took off her shoes and stockings and performed the feat bare-footed!

It is impossible to describe the feelings of the Japanese assembled.

To return to the servant question: Japanese women tie back the sleeves of their kimonos with a cord, as these long sleeves must indeed be a hindrance to a hard-working woman when scrubbing and cleaning. I was, however, warned never to allow my amah to tie up her sleeves in this fashion, as it is considered impolite for her to do so in the presence of the mistress. When staying in Wai-hai-Wai I remember one of the boys in the hotel who wore a pigtail, as was then customary with the Chinese, and who had tucked it into the pocket of his linen coat when handing round the dishes, which seemed to me a very wise plan to keep it out of the way; and I was much surprised to learn that this action had resulted in his dismissal so impolite was it considered to be.

My second amah was a merry, fat little person, of about eight and twenty, which is nearly middle age in Japan, and she was looked upon as quite an old maid! I called her Hanna, the Japanese for flower, as her real name was unsuitable. Her father was of the Samurai class, but she had gone into service among foreigners as a mere girl of fifteen. She proved to be a real treasure, most hard-working and good-natured. Her mother had died when she was quite a girl, leaving a baby boy in her charge, with the wish that she should make a dutiful daughter to her father. This charge she had most valiantly fulfilled, taking most of her earnings home so as to educate her brother. She went home every Sunday regularly, and if, during the week, I gave her any sweets, cake or fruit I would see these delicacies lying waiting on a shelf uneaten, and invariably wrapped in a little handkerchief (or furushiki), which it is customary to use in place of paper, ready to be taken home. These handkerchiefs are often lovely to look at, with the bright red glow of the sun woven into them, and various flowers and pictures. Japanese servants provide their own food, and any little gifts from their master's table are very much appreciated by them, so that the Sunday offerings which Hanna took to her father entailed a certain amount of self-sacrifice on her part.

How suitable was her name when one thinks of the little twigs and blossoms or tiny single flowers which invariably found their way into her room; these odd little flower visitors were her constant and often her only companions. She liked her European bed, but never seemed to use a chair. I can see her now, stitching away busily on a little raised straw mat, always happy and contented.

When first she came to me she could only speak a few words of English; when I left she could speak almost fluently; but her proficiency was only acquired by hard and often late hours of study. Her English was very amusing! With a serious face she told me a lady visitor had arrived whose name she had forgotten, but whom she described as " the lady with departed hair; " I instantly pictured a bald visitor, but, upon further inquiries, discovered she had her hair parted down the middle. Once she remarked that I could not go out as there was a " fox outside," which somewhat mystified me, until looking out of the window I discovered a thick fog! She studied English every night, sometimes as late as twelve o'clock, and once or twice I have been awakened by the sound of loud snoring in her room, and have found Hanna with an English book in her hand, lying curled up sound asleep on the floor. Considering that she got up at 6 a.m., and worked hard all day, those late hours were far too much for her, and I offered her an hour off during the day so that she could study; but this she refused, saying that her time must be solely devoted to me.

After I left she went to some missionary lady, as she wished to become a Christian. She certainly kept a watch over me as to my religion, and startled me once when I was in trouble by asking me why I did not speak about it to my God. "He will make it all right," said little Hanna, with a most childlike conviction in her mind. Whatever her creed may have been in the past, her life beautified any religion.

On my last visit to Japan, fairly recently, this little woman stood on the quay at Yokohama to meet me, and when a serious illness set in immediately after my arrival nothing would induce her to leave me. She sat up all night just like a statue, literally not moving a muscle lest the noise of her movements should disturb me. After my recovery she actually presented me with a priceless family heirloom, remarking simply that she and all her people wished to offer it as a proof of great thankfulness for my recovery.

As time went on I longed to weed out the innumerable attendants, and to make a big upheaval. But my only safety lay in working slowly, remembering the strong spirit of clanship which prevailed, more especially in the kitchen.

The Kagoshima men did not show any wish or adaptability for mixing with men from other provinces, and it was hard to find Englishspeaking servants among the men of the South. The latter are sea-faring men, strong, capable workers, and the duties of waiting at table in foreign style did not appeal to them. Nevertheless I made a point of securing Satsuma men and tried never to dismiss them, although it was often very difficult, for they were by nature fighters and warriors, regular rough diamonds, and not peculiarly suited to housework. I can see these new coolies now, on their first entering service, as they slouched along through the big play-room, flapping things with a little feather broom, by way of dusting. Every morning, as I went round the house on a tour of inspection, I came upon these coolies working, and at first they seemed dreadfully morose, as if they objected to the " foreign lady; " but their attitude gradually changed, and as on going my rounds I noticed and commended any bright piece of metal or polished glass they began to greet me with a smile. They had an annoying habit of always dusting the furniture before sweeping the floors. I tried to convince them that this was labour lost, and that after the floors had been swept the dust would settle again on ornaments and furniture, but they remained unconvinced and only strict discipline compelled them to dust the rooms after the floors had been swept.

It struck me that there was a great lack of perseverance and of steady work in the Japanese servants, and after showing them how to clean floors or windows I noticed they would carry out my instructions zealously for two or three days only, after which they would revert to their old routine.

There was one somewhat hopeless coolie who always was inclined to shirk his work. I often felt tempted to have him dismissed by the head gentleman as " impossible," but as he was one of the " clan," I steeled myself to greater patience and kept him on. One day during the war I heard a bellowing sound in the kitchen, and, asking what was wrong, I was told that a coolie was going to the Front and wanted to see me before leaving, but that owing to his inferior position it had not been permitted him to do so. I gave orders for him to be sent for. When he came my interpreter informed me that he said he had the happiness of being called to fight, and in all probability would have the honour of dying for his Emperor, but before he left he wished to ask my pardon. During his service as coolie he had hated his work and spoken rude things against me (the interpreter said he had called me a " cat "), and that now the time had come for him to go he was sorry. I said I would, of course, pardon him, and congratulated him on going to fight. A long time after, when the war had come to an end, this coolie returned and wished to see me again. He had a little china pot in his hand, which he had brought for me having been rewarded for some especially good piece of work. He said he had never known till he left what home life meant. Although merely a kitchen coolie who had only seen me for one or two minutes a day he thanked me kindly for my good influence, and said he had often thought about the " foreign lady," and that when he was fighting hard against foreign soldiers, " had tried to kill them gently for my sake."

I came across another instance of gratitude, in the case of a jeweller's workman. I had sent a long gold chain to be mended. On the day of sending it we had a bad typhoon, the wind being so strong as to blow over the handcart belonging to the jeweller's shop. My gold chain fell out of the cart unnoticed and was, consequently, lost.

One Sunday when starting for church two men came up to me, who proved to be the master of the shop and the man who had drawn the cart which had so unluckily become overturned. The master spoke English and told me plainly all that had happened, saying he would dismiss the man for his carelessness, and asking me what amends he should make for it. Looking at the poor culprit I saw such genuine terror on his face that, pitying him, I answered that there seemed no real blame, for such accidents would happen, and I begged that no more might be said about it and that everything might be forgiven.

More than a year after I received a most beautifully worked gold chain as a gift from this man. He told me that his master had intended to dismiss him, which would have meant serious trouble for him and his family, but that through my intercession he had been kept on, and had, therefore, saved out of his earnings money to get sufficient gold to make a chain, and had worked at it out of hours. He asked me to accept it as a token of gratitude.

It was about the same time that I had a very unpleasant experience one morning with some Turks.

Through my amah's limited interpretation I was told that two " church men " had come to see me. On going into the sitting-room, I found two Turks in clerical garb. They informed me that they were father and son, who had been converted to Christianity, and .they were touring the country as missionaries. I soon discovered that their object was to obtain money from me for their work. They were a very juvenile couple, so that their relationship seemed impossible, a fact which raised my suspicions, and made me feel that the cause for which they were pleading was not a genuine one. As soon as they saw that I was unwilling to give them money they became offensive in their manner, and ultimately threatening; one of them stood against the door and would not let me pass. Deeming it advisable to appear unconcerned, I changed my tone of refusal, and said if they would let me pass I would fetch some money, as their cause must be a worthy one to rouse such deep feelings in them. They granted my request, no doubt believing I would return with the money, and I rushed at once to the office to ask for help. The attendants, in spite of the fact that the interpreter was not present, grasped my meaning and themselves went to view the impostors, eventually managing to get rid of them by threatening them with sticks. At the same time they telephoned for the police, who soon captured these men and brought them up for trial, the result of which proved that they had for some time been procuring money under false pretences, and gaining their ends by threatening means.

This incident proved to be the beginning of a faithful protection afforded me by the attendants during the rest of my long stay in Japan.

CHAPTER XII

A REMARK is often made by my countrymen to the effect that the worst servants in Japan are invariably Christians, and, in a sense, this is perfectly true.

One of the chief qualifications given by a house-boy, when applying to a foreigner for a situation, is: "I am a Christian."

This is after the manner of the would-be Tommy, who, anxious to join the army at any cost, was asked by the recruiting sergeant as to his religious persuasion, and replied: "Well, sir, what are you short of?"

It is simply a matter of convenience: the wily Japanese boy calls himself a good Christian with an easy conscience, because he sees a better prospect of high wages, and an easier job.

But there it stops. On further acquaintance, and on going deeper into the matter, one finds that the boy is in total ignorance of the Christian faith. Many people with the easy-going idea of "leaving well alone" (if such a condition can be called well) go no further with the case, but content themselves with the statement that a lying and dishonest servant has been made so because his simple faith has been interfered with and he has been converted into a Christian.

Over and over again one hears such remarks, and often with the addition that " it is a mistake to interfere, since the climate and character of the Japanese are unsuited to Christianity." People sum up the situation as if becoming a Christian were in the same category as a change of diet or the adopting of some foreign social custom, but such is very far from being the case, as anyone who has had the good fortune to possess a real converted servant will readily admit. Japan needs a forcible religion to rule the individual life, and she herself knows this. At present there appears in Japan to be a rivalry between Christianity and Buddhism; Shinto worship, that is to say, " the way of the gods," is no longer a real religion among them, it has become a cult.

Japan tolerates all religions, and there are missionaries of about forty different denominations in the country. The English Catholic Church is strongly represented, and time only can prove the acceptance or non-acceptance of the living Truth.

It is often lamentable to see the want of tact amongst some of the well-meaning Christian workers. To a really sensitive people, such as the Japanese, tact is an all-important factor, although students of the Japanese language will tell you that for the word " tact " there is no equivalent. But the man with perfect sight does not need glasses, neither does he talk about his eyes: the Japanese language contains in itself the full meaning of tact, and every phrase expresses it.

I met in Japan a very delightful lady who was a missionary of the right sort. She had lived in the country and worked there for many years, and was loud in her praises of the goodness she had come across. She found her work intensely absorbing, and used to tell me that she often learnt from those she came to teach. On one occasion she was urging a young Japanese who wished to accept Christianity to read a portion of the Bible daily. The man's reply, so applicable to many of us, was: "I must either stop reading the Bible, or give up many evil things I am doing."

I have remarked before in these pages upon the earnestness shown by the Japanese students in study and self-improvement, but this is not confined only to the older students; and I have found this trait remarkably developed in quite young children. A friend of mine, who was teaching English to some little ones, told me that they showed not only gratitude, but real keenness in their work. She gave me a pathetic account of some little ones whose homes were too poor to provide lights for them to read by at night, and who sought the aid of their fairy fire-flies. Collecting them in great quantities, they placed them in little square boxes covered with muslin, and pored over their English books by the fantastic aid of their luminous insects. The same friend told me about some of her grown-up pupils, many of whom, though hard at work all day, would come to learn English in their free hours in the evening. They would also appear very early on Sunday mornings, never excusing themselves for absence.

On a certain day appointed for their lessons, some cause had arisen for national rejoicing, the result of this being that there was an unusual amount of sake drinking. But the men did not fail to come for their lesson at the usual hour. One, however, was not sufficiently clear-headed to benefit by the instruction and, after standing unsteadily for a time, eventually fell down heavily on to the floor. After that he was given to understand that this should be his last lesson. Very early the next morning, however, the man came to her full of apologies for what had occurred the previous night, and showed such genuine sorrow for his unsteady behaviour that his apologies were accepted, and he was allowed to continue coming to the class. It must be added that he was never known to transgress again, and he seemed to put all his energies into his work in gratitude for his forgiveness.

On one occasion I accompanied the Prince on a most interesting journey. We went up to Hokkaido, known as the North Sea circuit, to the provinces of the extreme north of Japan, where the race called Ainos are to be found. We broke our journey by stopping a night or two at various places, to which only a passing allusion can be made.

The first night, when stopping in a Japanese hotel, a fire broke out in a house adjoining, and spread rapidly The wooden shutters in the hotel were ail closed, and it seemed impossible to find the opening. The sense of being imprisoned, with the shouts of fire and rushing engines all around one, was rather alarming, but mercifully the hotel keeper soon came to our rescue and opened all the shutters.

On reaching Sendi, the first impression I can recall was the joy produced by the invigorating air, which increased more and more as we advanced. In visiting the shops there we found articles made out of a fossil wood which is obtainable from a hill near. These curios were less pretty than interesting. We saw a large stone tablet erected in memory of the men who fell in the Satsuma rebellion, which specially interested the Prince. The next stop was at Morioka, where the Prince presented me with one of the famous kettles for which this place is celebrated.

They are made of very heavy metal and are guaranteed never to get furred.

Not far from Morioka is a very well-known monastery called Chusonji, founded in the ninth century, which contains many valuable relics. The monks still use this monastery, but more as a hospitable refuge than for a life of prayer and meditation, or so at least it appeared, judging from a visit paid there by two friends of mine. Their experiences were most interesting and somewhat amusing.

These two ladies, accompanied by a guide, reached Hira-izumi station on their way up to Aomori, and finding it somewhat difficult to obtain a night's resting-place they boldly sent their guide on in advance to ask the monks to take pity on them and give them a night's lodging. After rather a long time their request was granted. They found the " guest room " most beautiful and comfortable. Having ordered a meal, much to their surprise a table was brought in and the meal duly served by the monks themselves, seven in number.

In the morning they requested the guide to prepare a bath. The bathroom was a large square wooden tank, boarded all round. In going to their bath my friends encountered endless fishermen, who had apparently come to this monastery from a far-off fishing village to make offerings. Like some of our own fishing- folk these men had seen and heard nothing of the outside world, and the foreign visitors were a cause of great excitement. Their interest was increased on hearing that the " foreign devils " were going to take a bath, and the men crowded round the bathroom, making full use of any peep-holes in the planks.

The guide afterwards calmly informed these ladies that these simple folk were under the firm conviction that foreigners had long tails, and were anxious to verify the fact!

Japanese fishermen, like our own, are superstitious and prejudiced, and at that time were not particularly friendly to outsiders; but since then they have learnt to put aside such superstitions and to understand us better, and I only repeat this story as one belonging to a bygone day.

On reaching Aomori I felt as if we had left Japan, for the whole city looked so foreign with its wide, straight streets. Salmon fishing is one of the chief attractions to visitors, and huge hauls of salmon are taken here; over eighteen thousand a day have been known to be caught not, however, of a large kind. A great deal of fish is exported from Hokkaido to China. Aomori is a great emigrating centre for Japan, and the Ainos are employed in a large fishing industry, for which Sapporo is also noted. I had expected to find myself in a wild, uncultivated country, and it was a great surprise to see there all the evidences of modern civilization, including tramway lines and electric light. So far we had travelled only by train, and had enjoyed all the comforts of a remarkably good service, but our journey next took us by a small steamer to Hakodate, a run of about six hours. This boat was essentially Japanese, including the food, and as the passage was decidedly rough it was not exactly a pleasure trip. Hakodate stands at the foot of a rock and people speak of it as the Gibraltar of the East.

After a short stay there we made our way up to Sapporo, where apartments had kindly been prepared for the Prince's use in a building having the appearance of a disused palace. The rooms felt as if they had long been empty and suggested barracks, which it was quite likely that they had been, as large numbers of Japanese soldiers and their families are quartered there. The most fascinating sight I saw in Sapporo was a number of little foals, some of them very young and very playful, belonging to a famous horse-breeding farm in the district. Another feature of interest here was a noted brewery, which we visited, going down into the vaults, which gave us a deathly, chilly feeling after the warm sun of the outer air.

Whether it was that I had only been a short time with Prince Shimadzu's family and was still ' an experiment," or whether it was the mere fact of being a foreigner, it was an unpleasing experience to find myself occasionally the centre of a curious and sometimes hostile crowd. At one place the pressure of people was so great as to break a part of my jinricksha, in spite of the attentive guarding of the policemen; ugly names were called after me, and I realized keenly that I was no longer in courteous Tokio.

Strange to say, however, when I found myself in the Aino village a sense of relief came. The natives showed very little interest, and were quiet and polite in their bearing, appearing both apathetic and unobservant. Indeed, on the other hand, I felt discourteous in my turn, and stood spellbound looking at them, for they are indeed original. They are called the " hairy Ainos" a most suitable name, for hair grew everywhere on them. There is something rather akin to our gipsies in these people. Some of the men were very handsome, finely built and broad chested; their features were not of the Mongolian type, but rather resembled Europeans. In spite of very bushy eyebrows they had gentle faces, and some of them had quite beautiful eyes, which were not only of a wonderful brown colour, but were dreamy looking and full of soul. The men wore their hair long and parted down the middle, and had wavy beards, calling to mind "Old Father Christmas." The women's figures were quite beautiful, and they held themselves upright with a dignity of carriage. They also had their hair parted down the middle and falling on each side of their shoulders. It is piteous that custom obliges them to tattoo a moustache on their upper lip and a corresponding one on their lower. One or two had their eyebrows joined by tattooing, and their hands and arms likewise were tattooed. They wore tan-coloured kimonos, the women's longer than the men's, and not girded in at the waist like the latter. The material used for them is made out of the bark of a tree which is split up and woven.

The village we visited stood quite away from all Japanese inhabitants, as the Ainos are not allowed to live among them, or in close proximity. The houses were not the least like Japanese dwellings, but had windows and a doorway. They were neatly built on high wooden piles, and were constructed of stout wooden frames, covered inside and outside with reeds. One thing noticeable was that each had a small outhouse attached to it, the roof of which was very low in comparison to the exceptionally high pitch of the main building. These dwellings looked very unsuitable for such cold climate as the Ainos have to endure in winter. I must not forget to mention that in this village there were poles stuck into the garden, with the skull of a bear placed on the top the bear being a sacred animal, which the Ainos worship. We met with no rebuffs on our visit, but on the contrary were most graciously received, and were even asked to go into one of their houses; but we did not avail ourselves of this invitation, contenting ourselves with looking in through the doorway. A thick mat of reeds was pushed aside, which evidently was used instead of a door we had previously been warned that it would be considered an insult to look into their rooms through the window. From this doorway the room appeared to be very dark, but we discerned a fireplace in the centre, and a large hole in the roof above for the smoke to escape. Over the fireplace was a huge iron pot, suspended from a chain hung in true gipsy fashion. We were told that the rooms are lighted by chips of forest bark, kept burning round the fire, and also by little wicks which are placed in dishes of fish-oil. When night comes the inmates sit in semi-darkness. There was a very European-looking shelf, after the style of a wall bracket, on which were placed numerous ornaments, mostly Japanese curios, and it is a very nice trait in the characters of these Ainos that they will not part with their treasures for any money. They will tell you, in their low, gentle voices, that they were gifts of kind friends to their fathers. So these ornaments are kept on a shelf, just as we keep our ornaments in the drawing-room.

Very interesting and curious was the form of their household gods, which resemble wands, to which a mass of ordinary curly wood shavings are attached. One was stuck in the floor, with shavings like branches projecting from either side. Another had the effect of a barber's pole, sticking out of the window placed there towards the east. By way of saluting us the men stroked their beards, and they all had a pretty habit of extending their hands and returning them to their faces in a gentle, waving manner. The women showed most beautiful teeth, and an Aino's smile ought to be proverbial for its charm. The tiny children wore no clothes, and one little baby was slung in a net on its mother's back.

On my return I ventured to ask many questions concerning these people. They believe they are all descended from a dog. They have no books as they possess no written characters, and in calculating cannot go beyond a thousand. They seem to be great sake drinkers, and use millet very much as the Japanese use rice. A baby has a seed of millet put into its mouth directly it is born, but I never discovered the reason.

Their treatment of the bear is most extraordinary. A baby bear is brought into the house and becomes a member of the family. The mother nourishes it in place of her own baby, who has consequently to be brought up by hand. When the bear gets older he is caged and kept there, until the season comes for celebrating the bear festival. One such feast was kept in honour of Prince Shimadzu and I was fortunate enough to be included in the invitation. We found two raised seats, somewhat after the style of thrones, prepared for us. They were covered with bearskins, a polite attention which is always offered to an honourable guest. We looked down on a half-circle of seated Ainos, who sat cross-legged (not like the Japanese), and in front of us was the patriarchal host, the chief of the feast, who, by way of salutation to the Prince, stroked his beard continually. The others gave the peculiar inward wave of their hands after extending them. One of the features of the feast was a loving-cup which was passed round, the little bear present sharing the honour, and drinking it quite elegantly standing up.

A wand with wooden shavings was waved over the bear. On our return home I was told that after this feast the bear was to be sacrificed. Though sacred in these people's eyes, a bear is put to all sorts of use. Not only is his skin sold, but his flesh is eaten, and his liver is used for making medicine. Yet chants are sung to him, and he is addressed as a god.

Our trip to Hokkaido indeed provided many subjects of interest and inquiry, and it forms one of the experiences indelibly written on my mind.

CHAPTER XIII

AS years sped on, the changes in the house and in our mode of living became more noticeable. The house itself was entirely refurnished and altered. The old office was converted into the linen-room, and a new one was built in a more suitable position. The two sittingrooms were knocked into one, and I was given a free hand as to the decoration, fittings and furnishings, all of which meant time and money. I gladly availed myself of sales of furniture at the various Embassies and Legations, but found that the idea of the Prince making use of any furniture which had seen service before was quite antagonistic to his attendants. Nevertheless this was the only way of procuring suitable articles, as the shops could only provide furniture of such an impossible style that many of my requirements had to be copied or recovered. I was allowed to have one or two treasures from the old home, to add to the new furniture; one was a most beautiful old Chinese cabinet, which had been presented to the children's father, and, with some of the genuine old Satsuma pots, the large drawing-room became quite beautiful.

These changes, however, were but of a passing kind, others more permanent could be seen. The Prince and his brothers soon rose above the average in athletics. Their training needed great tact and patience. The little brothers had first to learn to run and jump about, which meant many bruises and cuts for them. The youngest was the first wounded victim. He had a bad fall, which necessitated a day in bed as he was somewhat severely cut and bruised. Mr. Ibuski's indignation knew no bounds. He walked about the house literally growling. But I went on my way regardless of any disapproval and determined to develop their boyish inclinations to climb and run into danger. They seemed anxious to climb trees, so I forthwith offered a prize for the highest perch attained, disguising the quaking of my heart during the competition.

A good gymnastic master was also engaged, and I managed to get a few foreign boys to take lessons with the youngest Princes to encourage competition. They all made friends together, and threw themselves into the work, and soon became good all-round athletes.

The second boy took lessons in fencing, both pupil and teacher putting on heavy masks. The face-piece had metal bars over it, and the head-piece was made of thickly wadded material. They also wore a short skirt, a thick leather bodice and thick gauntlets, so that they were well protected except for the legs. The swords were strange sticks of spliced bamboo, folded together like the stand of a camera. The tips of these swords were protected by leather. From a conversation with one of the attendants I gathered that this game is regarded as a kind of mental gymnastics and is supposed to produce great self-control, and a high sense of honour. It struck me as being very hot and fatiguing work, apart from the heat of the clothing and mask, and I could not throw myself into the spirit of it. There was absolute silence on the part of the combatants.

The next step was riding lessons, and the boys did so well in these as to manage barebacked, spirited horses. A spill or two had to be endured, but there was no serious damage.

The shooting range was made in the garden, and a sergeant gave lessons. The Princes had wonderful eyes, and proved to be above the average as marksmen. Next came shooting expeditions, when they took their guns, accompanied by their gentlemen, and brought back a " bag " with pride and delight. Those days were real pain to me, the anxiety was so great, but I never let it be known.

We took a swimming master with us during the summer holidays. Day by day my charges had a slightly longer swimming record, and by the end of the holidays they swam well, and became more and more efficient every summer. Japanese students are keen boatmen. They hold their annual race in Tokio on the Sumida river, for which the students practise on halfholidays. It is a pretty sight to visit this river in the spring. Rows of cherry trees are planted on the banks, and when the blossom is in full bloom crowds of people both in boats and on foot may be seen, anxious to see their beloved cherry trees in full perfection.

We went up to Chuzenji, where there was a dangerous lake. But I was determined that the Prince and his brothers should distinguish themselves in boating, and it was not long before even the youngest child could handle an oar. The Prince had a more perilous training in sailing. I never let him take his brothers during the early stages, but accompanied him myself, so that his attendants could feel that I was risking my own life too. In looking back I almost marvel how I did it, so risky was this amateur sailing; but the result was worth it, as he was eventually able to compete in the races held on the lake by the diplomats and various members of the club.

On a visit to Wai-hai-Wai one summer with the three youngest boys, we were invited to a picnic by the Commissioner and his wife. The Goliath was in port, and a few midshipmen were invited to meet the Shimadzus. We had to fetch them, and I well remember how astonished the young men were to see the strength of wrist displayed by these little fellows. They pulled us along right merrily, and a good load we were! I felt very proud of my pupils.

Twice a year we had sports, which were held in the garden. It meant plenty of work for the attendants as well as myself. Many of the little Princes and Princesses and the pupils from the Gaksuhin were invited, besides the children of diplomats and others. We had sack races, potato races, threading the needle and the usual sports. It was a pretty sight to see the fair and dark haired little ones excitedly competing. Prizes were always given at the end by the Prince.

Another very enjoyable sport was ducknetting, for which Marquis Kuroda, a brotherin-law of the Princes, kindly invited us all once or twice a year to his beautiful park. The ducks are caught in huge nets, somewhat after the shape of butterfly nets. There are ponds and a canal, with very high embankments on either side, and peep-holes for watching the arrival of the ducks, which are attracted by decoys. The netter must use his wisdom and judgment so as to throw his net exactly at the right moment, and as this is not an easy thing to do, the excitement becomes intense. Directly the ducks have been caught their necks are wrung and they are eaten immediately, on the spot. A hibachi (or stove) is given to each person, who cooks his own meal, eating it with the much appreciated " Soy " sauce to flavour it. The flesh is very tender, but although the catching was most attractive, the eating of the bird was another matter, and the delicacy was wasted on me!

Duck-netting is of necessity an exclusive sport, as it requires not only a large extent of ground for a park, but quantities of water, which must be kept quite still, and it consequently involves very great expense. It was originally introduced solely for the Emperor and the Imperial family, and only one or two others in Japan have been able to indulge in it.

The diplomats receive a yearly invitation, and are selected a few at a time from the various Embassies. The honour of an invitation to the Emperor's duck-netting was kindly extended to me, but unfortunately, owing to circumstances, I was unable to attend.

A time came when the eldest of the three boys asked me pleadingly for a sword. It seemed to be only a natural request, but I referred it, as I did all such matters, to his eldest brother. The result was surprising, and gave me an insight into the solemn Ritual of the Sword. The Prince seemed to think it was quite out of the question for poor Junnosuke to have a sword, and showed that he was really hurt by the suggestion. When I questioned him on the subject he explained that the right to carry a sword, or even to possess one, demanded a certain nobility of character, and that the boy must prove by his life that he was fit and ready for such an honour: he must have the "warrior's mind." Eventually a sword was presented by the Prince to his young brother, but only on the understanding that it should not be unsheathed until he proved himself worthy of it. Certainly, a marked change was noticeable in him after he had received it. He lived as a responsible person.

Soon after this I was taken to the Nobles' Club, and entertained by one of the members. There was a sword dance, and in connection with it an allegorical play. It was most impressive, and I have never since been able to regard a sword as an ordinary weapon, so spiritual was its meaning, and have often longed that the Word of God might, in our land, have the same spiritual power.

A young Japanese nobleman, referring one day to a Christian's prayers, which he had been told were uttered in silence, confided to me that the sword which had been given him by his father, when a child, played the same part in his life. He told me that his father had called him to his side, when a boy of six years old, and suddenly asked him what he would do if an enemy came to fight him. " I would take up my sword," was the reply. This practical answer had so pleased his father that, in spite of his extreme youth, he had given him a sword. My friend then told me that he had always kept this sword in his room, and every night would stand holding it as he reviewed the past day and recalled what he had done unworthy of the sword. " What bad things I must cut through " was the expression he used. " I do also the same in starting the day, but no one must see me or know it."

There is also a beautiful custom of placing a sword on or near the body of the dead, the interpretation of which is the keeping away of evil spirits, so that the soul may rest in peace.

Few Europeans could understand with what appreciation the presentation of the late Colonel Calthrop's sword to Japan was received, unless they had been initiated into the spiritual significance of a sword to this nation. The fact that Colonel Calthrop had himself been presented with no less than six swords by officers of the Japanese Staff College (some of especially great age) is the strongest proof of their regard for this brave officer. After his death his mother presented one of his swords to the College an inspired action in view of the deep impression such a gift would make.

In the course of time there came a crisis in the Prince's life; he had learnt to think, speak and act for himself, and now had to make a vital choice as to his profession. Was it to be the Army, the Navy or the Diplomatic Service? One thing his guardians had all agreed upon was that he should make his own choice. They themselves necessarily held different opinions as to what this choice should be, seeing that they included brilliant men of both Services. I never spoke much to the Prince on the subject, until one day when he said with great determination that his choice had been made, and he meant to enter the Navy. From that date the Navy was his all-absorbing subject. But a fresh sacrifice had to be made, and one which affected me deeply, for he had to put himself entirely under the care of the Minister of the Navy, who would be his sole acting guardian, and whom he had to promise to obey in everything. One of the first changes was the appointment of Mr. Hirata as adviser to the Prince; my own work with him had to cease, and I had to take a subordinate place, which I should at once have disputed, but for my devotion to the Prince himself. I felt that by submitting to this most trying change I should help to make his position easier, but it proved to be a very difficult chapter in my life, as it put one of the attendants in power, and, consequently, affected all the others. For some years my rule had been more or less supreme, but now the attendants' power was to be felt.

At the very beginning of the Prince's naval career a question presented itself which was not only of vital importance to his own character, but was also one upon which the future naval training of Japanese princes would depend. How was he to enter the Service? As a fullblown lieutenant, which his princely birth could demand, or as an ordinary naval cadet? The subject was very complicated. The more conservative advisers desired the former, the more modern and advanced deemed it best that he should enter by competition. Needless to say, I longed for the more modern mode of entrance, which, fortunately, won the day. It was settled that the Prince should pass by examination into the Naval College at Etajima, and that he should go through the three years' training in exactly the same way as an ordinary naval cadet. This presented many difficulties. Would his health stand the strain such hard study as the competitive examination would require, and if he passed could he ever stand the hardships of the life?

Though my part in the Prince's education was not acknowledged from this time, yet I claim that the most important work I ever accomplished in Japan was at this crisis. His English was worked up in every spare moment, and a start was at once made to fit him for the physical hardships he would of necessity undergo. Hard beds, cold rooms, no carpets, Japanese food and long walks were gradually introduced; nothing of ease and comfort was allowed, and even the very cushions in the drawing-room were removed. I studied to make the home life harder and harder each day, but this side of his training never came under the Minister's notice, and was only felt by the Prince and those around him. Fortunately for me, Mr. Hirata was earnest for the Prince's good, and though there was much in my work in the past that he had resented, yet he tried in a measure to lessen the ignominy in which my new position placed me. It was a phase of anti-foreign influence in the Daimyo's household, but the nobleness of the Prince's character carried us all safely through; he constantly expressed gratitude for my past work, and asked me to carry it on steadily for his brothers' good; he never failed in courtesy, and I felt him a protector all through. In an extraordinary way he allowed no confidences from either myself or the attendants regarding the difficulty of my position, but the guardians helped me, and I feel confident that he was the acting spirit.

At length the day came for his entrance examination. Hard work and a strenuous life had already told on his health, and he looked very ill; but he went through it successfully, having been given exactly the same papers as the other cadets. When it was all over he ran hurriedly into the house, ordered a carriage, put on his best school uniform and drove off. I wondered at his haste and silence, but believed he had gone for an audience with the Emperor. Later on I discovered the reason. He had been given his diploma and was entered as a cadet at the Naval School, and the first thing that had come into his mind was to go to his father's shrine, and lay the diploma before the spirits of his ancestors. On his return he came straight to me and expressed his thanks for my help. Later on, as an acknowledgment of this, he presented me with most beautiful gifts, but the one I prize far beyond all was a little ring of plain gold, bearing his crest. To be given anything with the Prince's crest engraved upon it meant that he regarded me, in a measure, as one of his own house.

After this life of hard study he was allowed to enter into the festivities of the last few weeks of the year before he left for Etajima. A large dinner-party was given to all his guardians, and there was much speech-making. A very large public dinner was also given at the Naval Club by all the naval men of his province, and I was among the invited guests the one and only woman. This was a very gracious attention, and I thoroughly appreciated and enjoyed it. I sat among some of Japan's greatest admirals and heroes. Naturally, Japanese was the only language spoken, and in mentioning this I am reminded of a mistake which was caused by my ignorance of the language. My health was to be drunk, and I was advised when I heard my name, to stand up and bow in acknowledgment. I pricked up my ears lest I should, in the buzz of conversation, miss hearing my name. At last the moment came. My name was plainly spoken. Up I started, bowing, but only to fall back humbly into my chair, for the moment of toasting me had not yet arrived! It was only a passing allusion in conversation. An interesting ceremony was performed at this dinner. A portrait of the Prince's grandfather was brought out and raised as a shield behind him as he sat at dinner. Whether a prayer was uttered over him, or a vow was made, I do not know, but there was some great spiritual significance in this action. I returned from this dinner with not only a large bouquet, but a beautiful silver vase as well, engraved with the name of the President, Count Kabayama, and words of kind appreciation for my work.

Owing to the Prince's keen interest in all things naval his young brothers became quite absorbed in the Navy, and all were determined to become sailors. Every opportunity was given us of visiting the various squadrons when they were in port, and among our many visits was one to the Mikasa, afterwards gloriously known as Admiral Togo's flag-ship. This ship, after the Russo-Japanese war, was sunk by an explosion and was re-floated only by the exercise of untiring patience and at great expense.

On one occasion, when we dined on board one of the Japanese cruisers, I remember the sudden silence at table as the flag was lowered at sunset, and the solemnity with which the National Anthem was played by the band. Not a word was spoken, and all heads were bowed in silent reverence. The Japanese National Anthem grows on one. I learnt to love the sound of it and heard real music in the notes.

After a few weeks of festivities, however, the day arrived for the Prince to leave home for his new life in Etajima as a cadet. It was quite piteous to see his little brothers after he left, so dependent had they been on his words, and it was he who had added zest to all their games and fun. As for myself, I felt somewhat like a ship without a rudder, for though in a sense I had been entrusted with his education yet he had taken most of the responsibilities off my shoulders. Then, too, he had been a protector. For, working with men of such totally different ideas, there were always some objections to be overcome, some occasions when I was misjudged, and while the Prince was at home he stood as master. After all the care and engrossing thought I had given to his education it was hard to feel that he was to go entirely out of my life, not to be allowed to write to me, and perhaps not even to come back in the holidays. And there were some who whispered sadder things in my ears, telling me that the sons of nobility have not deep enough affections in their natures to remember a foreigner like myself. I had some heated arguments as to whether or not sincerity was a characteristic of the nation. All I remember is that when he left, the door shut behind him and I felt he had passed out of my life. In the lonely hours that followed I often asked myself what good seeds I had sown to influence him in his future work, and wished I could have done far more. He, on his part, had taught me endurance, and much that proved helpful in the future. As weeks passed on a letter now and again was received from him, and I discovered that no restrictions had been put on his writing, and when the first holiday came I was rejoiced to find that he was allowed back home. From the first day he left to the present time the lapse of years has made no difference. He has proved one of the best and truest friends that life has yet given me.

Not long after the Prince left for Etajima we paid a most interesting visit of two days to Marquis Matsukata's country place. It was some way from Tokio, we were about six hours in the train. This visit left a great impression on me, for it was the nearest touch of home life I had ever experienced in the East, and strangely resembled a place up in Scotland, with the delights and comforts of a house-party. The Marquis took much interest in the rearing of sheep and herding of cattle. Owing to the great heat the rearing of sheep had never been successful elsewhere in Japan; in fact, mutton was mostly imported from China. But grass had been most wonderfully grown and cultivated by Marquis Matsukata on his land. It gave one a strange feeling to look out of a window and see the sheep grazing and also to come down to breakfast and find an absolutely British meal, with a most kind and courteous hostess in the Marchioness, who, although she could not speak English, managed to express her pleasure at our visit through the interpreter, and to watch and care for all and every need we might have.

Amongst the many notabilities I met from time to time was the Marquis Tokudaichi, who was the constant and confidential companion of the late Emperor. In his capacity as the Grand Chamberlain to him alone was given the honour of driving with his Imperial Majesty, and whenever the Emperor drove through the streets of his people, the Marquis never failed to accompany him.

It was the daughter of the Marquis Tokudaichi whom Prince Shimadzu chose for his bride, and it is well known in Japan what a fortunate choice that was in every way. The marriage is a very happy one, the young Princess is much beloved and very popular, and they are the proud parents of a charming little family.

CHAPTER XIV

MILITARY experts and others have written fully on the subject of the Russo-Japanese war, therefore I will only give the impressions made on me, which were profound. If ever sorrows have been bravely and silently borne by a people individually, it was in those dark, sad days.

When I first arrived in Japan I noted the uniforms of the private soldiers with some surprise. They seemed so slovenly and showed no military smartness. I remember wondering then if this slackness would be carried into their work if they should be called upon to fight, little knowing that a war would come to prove both the thoroughness arid the smartness of Japan's soldiers. Now as to the awakening. In spite of war having loomed in the distance for some time it was a great surprise when one evening I was calmly told that it had actually commenced. In Japan important news is announced by the gogwai (the word gogwai means "extras "), who, as paper sellers, go round the streets ringing a bell incessantly, which brings the eager buyers quickly out of their houses; from the opening of the war to its end those bells seemed to be always ringing. My next impression was that when driving, a day or two after war began, the carriage was suddenly stopped and kept waiting whilst a few soldiers were being drilled so small a number as to be counted on one's fingers. It was a very narrow road in an obscure place, which had probably been chosen for practising the drill on account of its being out of the way. Daily these squads could be seen on the roads, drilling for all they were worth; and in the streets where trams were incessantly running they broke in horses, which was a most perilous proceeding for the passersby, although in no instance did I ever see a rider who was not master of the situation. Many of the horses were stabled in temporary sheds which were erected in the roads, and had the appearance of booths.

My next impression was of the great change made in the lives of the Princesses and the daughters of the nobility, including the Prince's sisters. They put down their carriages and used only 'rickshas, a most unprecedented occurrence, as, ilntil then, jinrickshas had been confined to the use of school children and attendants only. One of the Princesses, when going in the early morning to the war depot, actually used a tram for this purpose, and even discarded her lady attendant. She frequently washed the stained bandages of the wounded and disinfected them, which was amazing when one saw her beautiful, delicate little hands, and knew the seclusion and inactivity of her past life.

I was, naturally, most anxious that the young Princes also should feel something of the war, and in this the attendants tried to help me. The carriages were done away with, and changes in the food were also made, dispensing with puddings and dainty dishes. The Shimadzu family were only too glad to fall in with my suggestions, and the gentlemen, with their limited ideas, went even farther and proposed that their young masters should no longer wear uniforms of smooth serge, but should have them made of a coarse, thick material. They also urged my getting them the heaviest tramping boots for daily wear, such as were sent to the troops, but this I declined to do.

Our house was situated at a corner of a road where scenes of the war were continually passing before our eyes. The first which I remember, on looking out of my bedroom window, wa3 a long and endless line of jinrickshas. It looked like a black and white line of small carriages in the distance, but was in reality the wounded soldiers, all in white kimonos, being taken to the hospital. Twice a day they arrived by train, their wounds having been dressed and attended to by ladies of the nobility, who had been especially trained for this purpose.

Military funerals used to pass by almost daily, besides the processions of wounded men. Even now Chopin's Funeral March sometimes rings in my ears in connection with this time, so often was it wafted in at our windows. Very solemn and awfully sad were these scenes. One Sunday afternoon in May was most memorable, when the funeral procession of all the officers and men from the Hatsuse and the Yoshima passed by.

There was the funeral of Commander Hirose, one of Japan's noblest heroes, who, at Port Arthur, endeavoured to blockade the port by blowing up the ship on which he was in command. His glorious death influenced many young men in Japan, for he had lived contrary to his country's customs as regards visiting tea-houses and such places, and had strongly deprecated them; and after such self-sacrifice and bravery many of his old schoolmates and other students were unconsciously influenced by his opinions.

This funeral was an unfortunate occasion for me, because unwittingly I hurt some of the feelings of the mourners by breaking a Japanese custom. On hearing that the funeral procession of so great a hero was about to pass by I called the youngest Princes upstairs, telling them to stand at attention and watch from the windows, and explaining to them what a brave man Commander Hirose was. The next day I was informed by one of the attendants that Baron Yamamoto, the Minister of the Navy, had been horrified in passing and looking up to see my charges standing at the windows. It is thought very disrespectful in Japan to look down on the dead, and I grieve to say that the very object I had in view, of the young Princes showing respect and honour, had been regarded as an insult. The Minister, however, to whom I immediately wrote an apology, sent a very kind and understanding message in reply.

How easy it is for West and East to misunderstand one another, with such contrary customs! A propos of this, I remember that when going by train from the Shimbashi station in Tokio I was often astonished at the cold manner in which the relatives and friends of the various soldiers and sailors bade farewell to each other. On one occasion I got into a first-class carriage, where a naval officer was bidding his wife and child farewell. It was extraordinary to see the cold bow made by the pretty little wife to her husband. Certainly it was a very white little face which looked up at the carriage window, and lifted the child for a last farewell to his father. The officer took the baby's hand and raised it to his tiny cap as a farewell salute. It struck me as a loveless good-bye, with nothing demonstrative about it, and I recalled the many I had seen, comparing it with our own family farewells. The train steamed slowly out, and the officer stood saluting his wife and child, silent and calm. We were alone in the carriage, and he took a corner seat, furthest from where I sat. After a few minutes my eyes wandered towards him, and I saw that his face was as white as marble. He was holding up a newspaper by way of a shield, and almost as I turned my eyes away I heard one awful sob, and he fell back, to all appearances in a faint. It was a difficult position for me, as I could see that sheer grief of heart had produced it, but I sat still, as if I had seen and knew nothing, although I could not help feeling anxious lest he should go into a dead faint. Mercifully, he recovered and pulled himself quickly together, and I saw no more signs of grief. But I had learned a lesson. It was an example of a Japanese farewell, the very coldness of which was the result of the deepest emotion. How often I have longed to know whether he ever returned! My next experience was of receiving a message saying that a large number of sailors were to be billeted in the house. Each Japanese family was expected to put up men, belonging to various ships or regiments, who were passing through Tokio from the country on their way to the front. The number of men depended on the size of the house. There was a very large semi-Japanese room with a parquet floor and sliding windows which was used as a playroom by the children; it led from the diningroom, and the billiard-room was adjoining it. When first I received the message my heart sank. I pictured the place being overrun by men in a somewhat disorganized state, as they would have but a short time in Tokio for holidaymaking before going to the front. But again a surprise awaited me; they were never heard and rarely seen. No one would have known they were in the house unless they had opened the door of the " big room " (as we called it) and peeped through. I believe they were each provided with a sleeping mat, but I never saw anything being carried in or out. The Prince's second cook, who was kept exclusively for preparing Japanese food for the attendants and kitchen staff, managed to supply them with food. But from the day they arrived until their departure I never discovered how they were housed or fed, so little trouble did they give. I was anxious to give them a small entertainment, as it seemed a good opportunity for the young Princes to interest themselves on their behalf, and, with the help of friends, we had an evening of music and games. But they seemed constrained and ill at ease, as if they would rather keep quiet while under the Prince's roof, or it may have been that they were too seriously engrossed in the war and its necessary preparations. The games fell flat, and I did not attempt it again. Some time after the sailors left an equally large number of soldiers were billeted on us, and they, too, were quite unnoticed in the house.

Gradually the suffering due to the war became more acute, and we all longed to put out a helping hand. I tried again to lessen the daily comforts we enjoyed, but suspected that there was a certain amount of disapproval among the old-fashioned retainers, who still held to the belief that their Daimyo and his brothers were too great to be told of the sufferings of the poor and working classes. I resolved to do my share towards helping in the war, and wrote to the guardians, asking them to stop my salary for six months, and suggesting that the money should be handed to the Red Cross Society. This was gracefully accepted. When I left I discovered that the Prince had invested a like sum in my name, putting it into the War Fund and handing it back to me, with interest and a handsome present also added: so much was this small gift of mine appreciated.

In my diary, dated February 9th, 1904, I see the following entry: "I am sending 260 bags off to the front." These bags were made of paper, practically untearable, but extraordinarily light in weight. They were typically Japanese, both in themselves and in their contents, and contained among other things a tooth-brush, piece of soap, Japanese towel, chopsticks, packet of tobacco and a pipe. That they were appreciated was most evident. I copy here a letter and a post-card, which were sent me from the front, and were translated for me by my interpreter.

"To Miss HOWARD.

The weather is getting hot. I hope you are quite well. Since the war opened between Japan and Russia you have shown the deepest sympathy to our country and sent us the bags of consolation. They were sent through the hands of the Second Army and distributed among us.

I responded to a call at Hakodate on the 6th February last, to strongfold. Having accomplished the duty I left Japan last November for the front and landed at Tientsin in China on December 7th. Since then, I have been through the battles of Kokkodai and Mukden, but I was fortunate enough not to receive the slightest wound, by your protection and favour. I am grateful for it. We have still a long war ahead of us. In order to recompense your kindness, I intend being a mannurse in the Red Cross Society, and fulfil my duty in the work of saving the wounded soldiers. Hoping you are well,

HACHIJIYI OTA,

The head man-nurse of the 2nd Class in the Army.

Mukden,

Manchuria."

On the post-card was written:

"It is getting warm in Manchuria, but it is so much easier to live here. I hope you are well. I am quite well, so please feel easy. I cannot but feel grateful for the bags you sent us. I am using the contents every day in the camp. Day and night we are talking about it. Just to show my thanks I write this to you."

In connection with these practical and simple little bags I am reminded of a visit to the museum up at Port Arthur, after the end of the war. The few wants of a Japanese soldier compared with the European is most remarkable. The Japanese seem to have the gift of making something out of nothing. As an example of this, I saw a ladder which they made. Bits of bamboo and odd pieces of wood had been tied together with paper so as to form steps. In place of warm clothes they had used sacks with holes made for the arms to go through.

Their food was of the simplest, consisting mostly of barley and rice, a diet which had been especially ordered by the advice of Baron Takaki, whose great work I have already alluded to. He maintained that rice itself does not supply all that is necessary for nourishment, but that when barley is mixed with the rice and the two well boiled together it becomes both flesh and muscle making. This food was easily transported, and could be well washed before being cooked. Instead of heavy knives and forks, which European food requires, the use of chop-sticks considerably facilitated the food question in time of war.

Both the Y.M.C.A. and also the Salvation Army did great good among the soldiers in alleviating suffering, as well as by their moral influence. I cannot help referring, in this connection, to the great work done by the Salvation Army among the Japanese students, some of whom were living most immoral lives. They influenced them in a way that no other persons seemed able to do, changing their lives completely and winning their respect. I shall never forget the huge crowds which welcomed General Booth, and how they seemed to venerate him. There was also a Russian Roman Catholic priest, whose brave and loving work won many hearts. When the order was given for every Russian to leave the country, he asked to be allowed to stay on, and continued his missionary work with great self-sacrifice. I never learned his name, but the Japanese spoke most enthusiastically of him, and told me what splendid work he did.

A very impressive visit to one of the Red Cross hospitals revealed the universal love of flowers. Many soldiers returned from Manchuria during the war very badly frost-bitten. In one ward especially devoted to these poor men a lady took a nosegay of flowers. She told me that she would never forget the joy these flowers gave the soldiers. Most of them were fingerless and a few had stumps in place of hands, but they gave no thought to their pains. All they could think of was whether the lady visitor could manage to place a little flower firmly enough for them to hold in their fingerless hands. After giving each man a flower she looked round the ward, and saw each sufferer beaming with joy and gazing at the flower as if speaking to it.

In one ward of the same hospital she was taken to a room where the dying lay. The Sister told her to stand quietly in the ward for a few minutes. " You will not hear a sigh or a sound," said the Sister. " Our soldiers will never die except as heroes. They think a warrior must die in silence and not allow a sigh or sound to be heard." And it was so supreme silence reigned in this ward filled with many dying men. Thus pass the souls of all brave warriors.

As time went on the Japanese stoical endurance revealed itself more and more. A dignified silence reigned supreme amongst all classes, but the situation grew more and more tense. Most generous gifts were given by the nobility and others towards financing charities, and contributions to the War Fund were universally magnificent. Solid gold dinner services were thrown into the melting-pot, and costly heirlooms were offered for sale. Nothing was too precious to give away. One afternoon, when sitting alone, I had a visit from a little sad-faced lady of the nobility, and as we sat talking she mentioned that things looked very black and hopeless. I remember how depressed I felt after she left, and how I longed to question others as to the situation. I met my old friend the doctor, who, in his open, honest way, pronounced things to be serious. " But something will come to change it," he said, " you will see."

A very short time after this something great did come, which, without doubt, caused the final victory. It was an edict from the Emperor, speaking undying words to the people and to each individual. " Of you it is expected to accomplish the impossible." Yes, it had to be done. Defeat was impossible. How I remember the Prince handing me the translated words in perfect silence. The Japanese seemed to receive it with a breath of relief; they spoke as if victory was absolutely certain in consequence, and they proved it! Those words will go with me to the grave; they need thinking out and acting upon.

There is also a festive side of the war to be recalled, in its farewell dinners and celebrations of victories. Many dinners were given by diplomats and others, by way of entertaining the countless war correspondents who were not allowed to rush off post-haste to the front. It fell to my lot to see some of these visitors, who were much disheartened and not at all pleased with the long wait enforced upon them, and I was sometimes asked if I could not lend a helping hand and get them sent off. The Japanese hated refusing their requests; it was not characteristic of them to do so, and they often spoke about it to me with many regrets. But the way they were able to keep back every bit of news was surely one secret of their success.

CHAPTER XV

THE first celebration of victory in Tokio was on May 8th, 1904, when all the newspaper agents organized a lantern procession. We had a window over a bank, and saw everything beautifully. The scene was like fairy-land with all the different Japanese lanterns and brilliant colouring.

The month following was a busy one for me, as the Prince gave two farewell dinners, one for the Army and the other for the Navy. As the Manchurian army was about to leave for the front, Marshal Prince Oyama, his staff, and many celebrated generals were invited. They all appeared in full-dress uniform, with a perfect blaze of orders, and the whole affair was most brilliant. The second dinner was given in honour of H.R.H. the late Prince Yamashina, at which very celebrated admirals and others were present. This dinner seemed much merrier and less rigidly ceremonious than the former, it may be from the fact that most of the guests spoke fluent English. They were full of fun, and I much enjoyed the evening.

On the fall of Port Arthur early in the following year (1905) two celebrations in commemoration were given in Hibiya Park, Tokio. The illuminations were perfectly lovely and all the spectators behaved in a quiet, dignified way. The crowd showed little excitement. At the end of the war we went down to Yokohama to see the Naval Review. It was a great sight to see the Emperor, on a cruiser, passing through the huge circle of warships. The Prince did not accompany us, as he was on the Emperor's ship.

A grand military review was also held by the Emperor up at the Aoyama grounds. On this occasion he was mounted. We were invited to Princess Oyama's tent, where we could see everything perfectly. Nothing, however, impressed me so much as the garden party given by the Prince in the grounds of his Japanese house in Tokio. It was in honour of Admiral Togo after the war, and as it was exclusively Japanese I felt it a great compliment to be among the guests. It was a memorable sight. The Japanese are very proud of their gardens, one peculiarity of which is that on whichever side you look the view is totally different. Small stone bridges and lanterns, pagodas, summer and tea houses, with little hills and vales, are all to be found, adding to the prospect. On this particular occasion the chrysanthemums were in full bloom, and the garden was a mass of brilliant flowers, which, with the uniforms of the men and the gay kimonos of the women, made a brilliant and beautiful scene.

On fete days little girls are dressed in the brightest colours, generally red; they have patterns of large flowers and the family crest woven in their kimonos, except in the case of a small princess, when the imperial crest of the chrysanthemum is embroidered. They generally have a bunch of artificial flowers placed in their hair. Their elder sisters and the young married ladies wear the usual black ceremonial kimonos, with white vests and crests. By way of jewellery a brooch is worn to fasten the narrow corded waistband which goes round the obi, and they often wear most beautiful rings on their delicate little hands. Intermingled with the various colours there was a blaze of gold, for some of the silk obis worn were thickly woven in gold; they must have been very heavy and many were valuable heirlooms.

There were two naval bands, and in the course of the afternoon the guests, including the ladies and children, fell into line, marching behind one of the bands two and two, which is an old custom of the Prince's province. I can picture them now, marching to the music up and down the little hills, a moving mass of gold and colour. There were a few wooden seats with red blankets on them, placed at various corners of the garden. At five o'clock there was a sit-down high tea, and towards the close of the entertainment the hero of the nation and chief guest of the day, Admiral Togo, was chaired and given three tossings, that also being a custom of the province. The Prince received the same compliment. Before leaving we were each presented, as a memento, with a little china sake cup bearing the Prince's crest on it and the two flags of the Army and Navy crossed in the centre. Few Europeans have been fortunate enough to be present at such a purely Japanese function, especially on the commemoration of such a splendid victory.

Shortly afterwards I had an opportunity of seeing something more of Admiral Togo, as I sat next to him at an entertainment, and I was struck with the wonderful expression of goodness and peace on his face. One meets with such a look on the faces of some of our heroes of to-day, on their return from the front and the frightfulness of battle. It is as if they had had " a peep beyond " into the other side. Such was my impression of Togo, the Nelson of Japan, and the father of the Japanese Navy, the efficiency of which stands second to none, and which comes in strength as third only amongst the Allied Powers.

His career began at the early age of sixteen, when he was sent to England, where he served on board H.M.S. Worcester and afterwards studied at the Thames Nautical College, Greenwich. Thus he became one of us, and English influence followed him through life; it showed also in the other Japanese naval officers, very nearly all of whom spoke English and many of whom had received their training in our Navy.

In Admiral Togo I saw the man who commanded the fleet in the Japanese-Russo war the man who bombarded Port Arthur, who hid his ships for three months pending the arrival of the Baltic fleet, and who finally completely routed the Russians, though greatly outnumbered by the enemy.

During the long waiting-time the people and papers were full of questions. " Where is the fleet? " " What is it doing? " " Is it proving no use to us? " " Are they all asleep? " Everyone was blaming them! But that had no effect on Togo, who did not intend to be driven, and waited silently until the right moment.

When it came he knew it, and struck valiantly.

At the time that I met him his laurels were still fresh upon him and I hold that event as one greatly cherished in my memory.

In the autumn of 1905, after the victory and its many celebrations, Admiral Togo paid a most impressive visit to the Aryoyama Cemetery, where he went to address the spirits of those who had fallen in the war. Everyone who was present must have been impressed by his silent reserve, and have felt him to be a man of deep thought and religious feeling. The words of his address to the spirits were very remarkable and spoken in a most poetical form.

He tells them that " the whole city goes out, with peaceful heart, like that of a child," to meet them. He refers to their courage and the envy which " the glory of their loyal deaths have won." He tells them that the secret of their success was through " forgetting themselves," and expresses a belief in reunion with the dead when he says that " their families will wait for them at the gates of their home."

This touches a very sympathetic note to many of us at this present time, when we know so well what " waiting " means in our deepest grief and solitude.

That the spirits of the dead visit the home is so firmly believed among the Japanese that it is very rarely a family moves house within a few months after a death. They fear lest the spirit return to find the old house empty.

During the war many hundreds of men went out from Hirosaki, very few came back. It was a scene not to be forgotten; when the handful of heroes returned to their native town the assembled crowd received them with admiration and interest, but in absolute silence, for to the Japanese the dead alone are heroes.

This reverence for their dead is shown by the fact that the smallest portion of the body is regarded as sacred. At that time seven hundred widows of the men who had fallen went to receive (with all reverence and perfectly controlled grief) a small box containing the hair of their beloved ones; and after the ceremony these sacred caskets, with their contents, were laid to rest with full burial rites.

After Admiral Togo's great victories he still remained in Tokio in his little obscure house, with his name notified on the outside by a little wooden slab just like any other ordinary Japanese citizen.

To understand this great man thoroughly we must throw ourselves into the spirit of the Shinto creed. Shinto worshippers believe the dead never die, and that their spirits return to earth. They become deified. Amongst the dead there are three classes. In the first are those who by relationship belong to us, and with whom the Japanese commune daily in the little home shrine which is in every house; the second is composed of those connected with the old feudal days, the spirits of their masters, as it were; and the third of those who exercise a national influence over the whole land of Japan and over each citizen the Imperial ancestors of the Emperor.

The Japanese believe that the spirits of the departed have supernatural power, which they can exercise to help us and protect us; and those left behind have a duty to perform, in keeping them ever in remembrance and in acknowledging any special help or benefit coming from the spirits. Thus Togo lived, taking no credit to himself of his wonderful victories. He himself was no greater than before, but ascribed all his victories to the spirits of the Imperial ancestors.

The signing of the peace in America was the cause of very serious riots. The newspapers seemed to minimize the importance of them, but the experiences of those who were in the capital at the time will not easily be forgotten. They started in the Hibiya Park, where the celebrations of victories had been held, and it was indeed a sad sequel that riots should break out there. Directly it was known that the peace terms had not given satisfaction to some of the people the police had closed all the entrance gates of the park early in the morning, so as to prevent the people entering. Apparently this step had been taken by the police without the consent of the city authorities, and this aroused the anger of the mob. They believed the Minister of Home Affairs was responsible and made a rush on his house to burn it down.

I happened to be near there at the time, accompanied by Hanna. We knew nothing of what was occurring in the park, nor of their intentions towards the minister. I only felt something was wrong. Crowds seemed coming together, and I noticed that one or two people seemed inclined to be rude and angry towards a foreigner like myself. Hanna quietly advised that we should return home in all speed, which we managed to do. During this time the people fought their way through the park gates, burning part of them, and upon entering the grounds they started letting off fireworks as proof of their entrance. This added to the excitement and angered the mob, and the police, on interfering, were violently attacked and were obliged to draw their swords in self-defence; the result being that one or two people lost their lives. Towards the evening the rioting increased. They began to throw all the blame on the Prime Minister, Count Katsura, whose house was next to ours. They aimed at killing him and burning down his house, but precautions were wisely taken and the house was guarded by soldiers inside and surrounded outside by police.

The house of the Minister of Home Affairs was, however, burned down, and the excited mob stopped all fire-engines from going to the rescue, throwing down the firemen, one poor fellow being killed. After this the mob set fire to many other buildings in Tokio and burnt several tramcars. In spite of all precautions the lodge at the entrance of Count Katsura's house was burned down. Just at the crisis of affairs a Japanese missionary was misguided enough to hold a meeting and address the mob on the advantage of peace, which naturally added fuel to fire, and so irritated the rioters as to lead them to attack the Japanese Christian churches, and also to make an attack on the Russian church. But, fortunately, soldiers were at hand who were commanded to fire on the mob, using blank cartridges for the first shot, and announcing that the second shot would be a live one. This completely quelled the mob, and they turned from frenzy to friendliness, ending in a hearty " Banzai! " for peace. There were scarcely any foreigners in Tokio at this time, as they were mostly away for the summer holidays; in fact, someone told me I was one of a very few. One morning, I walked up towards the British Embassy and met two very insulting coolies on the road, who spat at me continually, shouting angry words. I was forced to walk on, as there was no house along the road to shelter in, but it was a horrid experience. It was, on the whole, quite a time of terror, for so many of the police had been wounded, and burglars took advantage of this fact. A circular was sent round to each householder asking him carefully to guard his house owing to the scarcity of police. Posters were put up by the rioters, saying that if any house were lighted up after nine o'clock they would attack it the object of this being to have the town as dark as possible for plundering purposes. But typical of Japan's ways of working there seemed to be a silent and mysterious grip which completely quelled the riots, and after a few days of martial law the usual peace and happiness once more reigned in the capital.

CHAPTER XVI

IN 1907 I was informed in a letter from the Prince that his brothers and myself were all to visit his province, which we had wished to do for a long time. It was an experience never to be forgotten. My charges were always bad sailors, and the interpreter and amah hopelessly so. The two gentlemen made great efforts to keep up; but it was a choppy sea, and we all succumbed. The boat had been especially chartered for the use of our party and it had apparently been expected that we would bring our own staff of servants. Not, however, knowing this, we were quite a small party, and the want of a steward and stewardess proved very trying. There was no one to wait on the young Princes; the two women were in a state of collapse, and the gentlemen's efforts were at zero. Everyone lay helpless. On reaching Hosojima, I managed to give them a cup of Liebig, but we were ill all night.

One of the boys turned faint, so I had to get up, and found it a good cure for mal de mer.

Hanna failed me this once! She sobbed and groaned between her attacks. Finally, about three-thirty, we sighted Kagoshima, the capital of the province of Satsuma. Our boat was gorgeously decorated in honour of the Princes, and flags were flying everywhere. There were masses of people; the hills looked black in the distance, so dense were the crowds. Many relations were at the landing-stage, and a serious amount of saluting and exchanging bows, together with introductions, had to be gone through. The boys were limp and weary, and we all felt fairly spent. But the soft air and glorious scenery put fresh life into us, and we started immediately in jinrickshas to visit their father's shrine before going to the house. The behaviour of the crowd was indeed noticeable very different from what I had to endure five years previously when travelling up to Hokkaido. No policeman accompanied us, and everyone seemed quiet and pleased. As the Princes' jinrickshas passed, the spectators fell on their faces, bowing after the old custom.

How can I describe the ride up to the grave or the beauty of the sacred spot itself! The cherry trees were in full bloom. Stopping at a steep hill, cut into steps, we walked up to the shrine, which was in a, quiet corner, looking down on to the sea a very paradise. The nightingales were singing most beautifully.

To reach the spot we had to pass through two gates, or torris, which are always to be found in Shinto temples where ancestors are worshipped. An attendant asked me to go up to the grave, saying " the spirits would be so pleased at my going to visit them first, before going to the Prince's house." (This was interpreted.) Arriving there I made my bow, and we shortly returned to our 'rickshas and went straight to the house.

The site on which it was built was quite ideal, and the garden most beautiful, with Japanese stone lanterns dotted about, many of them strangely shaped. Huge rocks had been placed there, resembling some sacred animal, such as the tortoise or the crane, and there were some perfectly fascinating small cascades through which the water fell from the surrounding hills.

The house was furnished as if for a fairy prince, with aged dwarf cherry trees bent in the queerest shapes and bursting with blossom, and here and there golden screens hundreds of years old. If only they could have told their tales of the heroes whose records they proudly bore!

It was a great pleasure whilst sitting at meals to have before one the vista of this wonderful garden, and I enjoyed the sight of it almost as much as the food, which in itself was both varied and original. Kagoshima is renowned for its fish, and is also famous as being the first place in Japan where potatoes were planted, the kind cultivated being very sweet and pink-fleshed. Most fascinating cakes are made from a local seaweed. When in Tokio boxes of oranges, pumpkins and melons were sent from Satsuma for the use of the Princes, also venison and boar, the province being noted for boar hunting.

From the moment of arrival until the very end numerous visitors were coming and going, making separate calls on the young Princes and myself. No hour was too early, and an uninterrupted meal was impossible, for Japanese etiquette forbids the excuse of being " otherwise engaged." This amounts almost to slavery, and no protection whatever is afforded one, as the visitors appear more or less singly, and never on a stated day en masse. Among the earliest of our callers was my old friend, Mr. Ibuski; he seemed quite friendly and pleased, and brought with him a beautiful little gift.

Our second jinricksha ride was made to the grandfather's grave, and from there we continued a circuit of visits to ancestral tombs. At each tomb a beautiful Satsuma china pot with the Shimadzu crest was to be found, and a little mat for each child to prostrate himself. We came to a stone terrace where there was a stand for holding rice and a large mat in front of it, and Prince Junnosuke told me that this was an opportunity afforded them for worshipping all the spirits, as time prevented their visiting them each individually.

We made an expedition to the place where Admiral Togo and General Kuroki were born. There we found trees which had recently been planted by Prince Arthur of Connaught and his suite in appreciation of these noblemen. It was wonderful how many places of interest we visited in so short a time, and when the day of leave-taking came we all had a feeling of depression, in spite of the many gifts and flowers showered upon us.

We left the house about 4 a.m., but this did not lessen the crowd that came to bid us farewell. It was quite enormous, and I found myself in great demand with people who wanted to shake hands; some ladies expressed their gratitude for my work with the Princes with tears of emotion. British flags were everywhere. It was a pathetic sight to see the farewells exchanged between the people of the province and their young lords. The former had a quiet, resigned look on their faces. Several attendants accompanied us by train for about half an hour, and as we passed the stations the crowds were quite dense; everyone wanted to see the children.

After a three hours' journey we reached Yoshimadzu, a very dirty little place, with crowds of poorly-clad spectators. Everything had been duly prepared for our arrival. There were jinrickshas with three runners (two as tandem and one push-man behind), and three omnibuses for our luggage; the leading runner carried a little cane in his hand, which he waved to clear traffic and point the way, When we reached the province of Kumamato a policeman and two gentlemen were added to the long procession of jinrickshas. We made a steady run of about two hours on an exceptionally good and flat road surrounded by mountains, with visions of barley and rice fields everywhere. It was somewhat fatiguing as there were crowds of spectators more or less all the way. Schools lined the roads, and as the Shimadzu Princes passed by most of the lookers-on prostrated themselves. It was necessary for me to watch carefully and distinguish when the salutations were exclusively for the Princes, and when I was included.

As we gradually got into the heart of the country a change came. The people adopted the very old-fashioned customs, and hid themselves behind trees and mounds and even lay in ditches, doubled up. They must not be seen by the Princes. We passed several cemeteries with endless flags on bamboo sticks (a name on each stick) where soldiers who had fallen in the war had been buried.

Our first stop was at Kakuto, the crowd there was very dense. We found a charming house, which at first we mistook for a hotel, and I started giving orders through the interpreter. But we fortunately discovered it was a private house, lent to the Princes for the occasion. Everything was beautifully arranged, a luncheon being prepared upstairs for the Princes and myself. Soon after luncheon we started off again, a very long procession of jinrickshas, to which another gentleman had been added.

We made a long, steep ascent, and as we circled higher and higher up the mountain a marvellous view revealed itself. The only drawback was the dust, as a very strong wind was blowing.

We reached Kumamato Ken (or province) and stopped to take tea in a temple. The crowds were indescribable, and three policemen came and stood by to guard us, although in reality there was no need for this, as the people were quiet and well-behaved. After tea we made another run of an hour and a half, and reached Hitoyoshi, where the crowd of people looked poor and not as clean as usual. We put up in a Japanese hotel, which might have been renowned for its noises. I abstained from using the bath, all privacy being out of the question. The next day we started early in the morning to go down the rapids, a journey which took nearly nine hours. It was very cold and foggy, but we regaled ourselves with a large meal, and set off in two boats which were in readiness.

As we approached the landing-place, having been already sighted by the police stationed on a bridge, we were surrounded by barge-men, and were afterwards hurried to Yatsushiro station, a small wooden house with open windows without glass. The curiosity of this crowd to see a foreigner was decidedly embarrassing to me, but the police kept the people back.

We next arrived at Hakata, where several officers met the Princes, and we were quickly packed into jinrickshas for a ride. I shall never forget it. We literally flew! A police officer headed the procession, holding in his hand a lamp with an official notice on it, which cleared the way. How we circumnavigated the corners remains a marvel, and the memory of it haunts me yet; but we all reached the hotel safely, and left again the next morning for Moji, where the usual kindly crowds awaited us. The Governor was at the station, where chairs had been thoughtfully placed.

Moji is not an attractive looking port, and was a great contrast to the lovely scenery through which we had passed. Getting on to our boat, we made a pleasant trip to Shimonoseki, and put up at the European hotel there on our way to Etajima.

Amongst the many strange and wonderful things I have come across, one of the weirdest and most fantastic was to be seen in the waters around the Straits of Shimonoseki. Here we saw gigantic crabs, quite unlike any I had ever seen before. On their huge backs were clearly depicted human faces, the expressions being so full of misery and suffering that it gave one a feeling of depression. The legend of the people is that these crabs were formerly soldiers who lost their lives in the battles of past ages between the two important Houses in the Straits. It appeared to me to be but a poor reward for their valiant conduct, but the idea was deeply rooted.

In more recent years a treaty of peace, putting an end to the Chino-Japanese and Korean war, was signed at these Shimonoseki Straits.

At Etajima further interest and pleasure was afforded us in a day spent at the Naval College, where the young Princes had the joy of seeing their eldest brother again. Etajima is a small island in the Inland Sea which is given up to the college, and is quite near to the important arsenal of Kure. The system of training for the Navy is very different from the English one, as the cadets have already graduated, and take their three years' course much as our men do in the universities. They do not go to sea until they are over twenty years old, when they then go for a cruise round the world, and return as naval officers to an academy in Tokio for a course of gunnery and torpedo instruction. Nevertheless, this three years' training in Etajima gives them a fair start in the discipline and hardihood necessary for a life at sea. Many of them enter physically delicate and within a few months show a remarkable change in their whole physique.

We spent a most interesting day there and received untold kindness, and my charges returned with a greater longing than ever to follow in their brother's footsteps.

About the time of our visit the cadets of the third year were competing in boat races round the island of Etajima, which is about forty-five miles in circumference. They enter with great keenness, and are allowed either to sail or to use oars. The object is to accomplish the feat within the shortest time.

They all started in the early morning. The first men in arrived at eleven o'clock at night and the last at four in the morning. They are divided into various classes or buntai. There is a strong esprit de corps among the cadets. Defeat in no way hindered them from cheering the victors in all their sports. Their manners were more like those of full-fledged officers, and in spite of a hard life the rough school-boy seemed to have vanished. I had a kindly welcome from one or two of the Prince's friends whom I knew best, and they even showed appreciation which I shall never forget at the delight I felt at seeing them again. One of the cadets wrote me an English letter during the war. After writing "Many are suffering at the front for the country's sake," he commented on the college training, and at the end of his letter described his idea of the duty of a naval officer in the following words: "An officer in the Navy must be truthful and obedient and work for a higher cause." Certainly their training seemed to aim at this, and from the start to the finish life in the Japanese Navy maintains a high standard of thoroughness and honour.

A British squadron under Admiral Moore had lately paid a visit to Miyajima, which is within a short distance of the college. The cadets, therefore, had the opportunity of visiting some of the ships, including King Alfred, the Kent and some torpedo-boat destroyers which greatly interested them. The scenery of Miyajima itself is perfectly beautiful. It might truly be called a paradise on earth. In approaching the island a torri, or Shinto gate, can be seen, which is built out at sea and appears, with the shadows it casts, to be a labyrinth leading to a fairy kingdom. Certainly its portals do not open into death, for there is a strange law in the island which forbids people dying there.

Neither birth nor death are admitted. Should, by chance, a baby be born there, both the mother and child are sent over with all speed to the mainland; and should a sudden death occur the body is immediately removed. Deer wander about quite tamely, and flocks of doves fly round the temple; many of them will come and settle on people's shoulders and eat out of their hands. No dogs are ever allowed on this island. The men from our ships must indeed have found it a haven of rest.

CHAPTER XVII

IN October, 1905, our second destroyersquadron paid a most memorable visit to Japan, to commemorate the renewal and extension of the Anglo-Japanese Alliance. On this occasion they went to Kagoshima, and indeed no spot could be more associated with the Navy than this province, which owed a great deal in the past to the Shimadzu family. To quote from a document which was presented to me just before Prince Shimadzu entered the Navy, " It was Prince Nariaki who had been a pioneer in establishing the progressive policy of Japan, and carried its principle into practice in his own domain, especially in the matter of military and naval affairs."

The squadron had arranged to arrive at Kagoshima on October 22nd, so as to commemorate the centenary of Trafalgar. The city was gaily decorated, and the Mayor and several' people of importance steamed down the bay to meet the ships, and gave a most hearty welcome to Captain Charlton. On their arrival the Governor paid an official visit to the Hecla, and nineteen guns were discharged; and when Captain Charlton and many of his officers and men came on shore glorious shouts of "Banzai!" resounded on all sides.

Their visit was the occasion for several brilliant fetes, and proved a friendliness between the men of both navies that will not easily be forgotten.

The description of the mission to Japan of Prince Arthur of Connaught, in order to bring the Garter to the late Emperor, has been so well &nd fully reported that I need not attempt any further descriptions, except to mention that the preparations in the Japanese Court were on an extraordinarily large scale. I remember one of the Court officials telling me he had been so hardworked that it had not been possible for him to go to bed all night, and that he had found it a very good plan to wash his face in iced water this being an unsurpassed method for overcoming sleep!

The Prince's visit was indeed a boon for the shops and dressmakers, and alas! some went near to robbery things were at such fancy prices. One French dressmaker sent in a bill of 17 for merely making up an evening gown, the silk having all been given her. White gloves were at a premium, as the boat which was to have arrived with a fresh supply did not bring them in time. The climate of Japan makes it impossible to store gloves in quantities, though many ladies manage to lay by a stock by keeping them in large glass bottles in napthaline, but even so they get more or less affected after a time. I found that the only available gloves were in Yokohama, and their price was 14s. a pair! But Prince Arthur's visit proved to be so much appreciated and was such a success, from both the Japanese and our own point of view, that such trivialities were of no consequence.

Japanese tailors were at this time in great request. They are ingenious enough to copy a model exactly, and if a French gown can only be secured and handed to a tailor it can be duplicated perfectly, with the additional advantage of costing less than a quarter of the original model. It is, however, almost impossible for the Japanese artistic eye to duplicate without just one touch of originality, and the tailor, who soon experiences the wrath of his lady customer if he does not strictly carry out her commands, will in all probability pin on a queer little piece of ribbon, or sew on a button, of a colour greatly in contrast to the gown! The tailor I employed was quite a treasure in his way. On my leaving Japan he wished to prove the progress he had made in English by his interviews with me over my garments. He wrote to wish me ' bon voyage," adding respectfully he trusted to hear " Lady v reached terra firma with good "bodice. ?J

Prince Arthur made a tour of inspection to Prince Shimadzu's province as his guest, and quite won the heart of his Japanese host, who, however, did not at first seem to relish the idea of entertaining the royal visitor. He was, indeed, quite prepared to dislike him, and the fact that his mother was a German made him more than ever inclined to feel unfriendly towards him. It was on his return from Kagoshima, where Prince Arthur had been staying as his guest, that I heard how closely in touch the two young men had been. Prince Shimadzu was quite enthusiastic about him. " He doesn't like the Germans any more than I do," said Prince Shimadzu to me. ic He says the only redeeming thing in all Germany is his mother. If it weren't for her he would hate them. I like Prince Arthur for this," he added, " that he is fond of his mother."

I believe much sympathy existed also between the two on the subject of speech-making. During my various travels I have found many princes affected with pains below their chest both before and after speechifying, but as to whether these Princes suffered in this way it is neither my business nor the reader's to speculate!

It is quite a question whether Prince Arthur realized what critical eyes were upon him always. Everything he said and did was weighed; and let it be said that the result was all to his credit. One of the courtiers, in speaking of him to me, said that it was a proof to him what great value a good mother is even to a Prince and that Prince Arthur seemed to know what home life meant. The Japanese nobility had a great terror of card playing and whisky drinking for their Princes and young noblemen; they constantly expressed their dissatisfaction that in Tokio so much Bridge playing with high points went on among diplomats and the foreign community. They had always a dread lest their own Prince should be drawn into it, and they pronounced Prince Arthur's influence in all these respects as being so good.

In one hotel we were staying at up in Miyanoshita a young duke from home had greatly disgusted and shocked the Princes' gentlemen by his dissipations. He certainly could not have realized the bad turn he was doing to British prestige. One lady remarked that Prince Arthur was very different from an Eastern prince who had once visited Tokio, and for whose constant companionship they had to take untold trouble in finding pretty Geisha girls and such-like entertainment. Prince Arthur certainly fulfilled his mission in the eyes of the Japanese, and acquitted himself nobly and with royal dignity.

One morning during his visit to Tokio a severe earthquake took place, the worst I had ever experienced. The brothers were all at school, and I remember standing in the doorway in the schoolroom, very anxious as to their safety, but knowing there was nothing to be done.

When an earthquake comes it is usual to stand between two door-posts, for if the house should fall the chances are that by so doing you get some protection over your head. However, it soon passed and nothing serious happened.

On the same afternoon a grand concert took place in the Academy of Music in Uyeno. It was given in honour of the Royal visitor, and was attended by all the Imperial princes and princesses, the latter being in European dress. The Empress was very ill at the time, but out of thoughtful consideration for our Prince, no public notice had been taken of her illness. We went in quite a large party, the Prince, his two brothers, and one of his sisters, whom I had been asked to chaperon, together with two gentlemen attendants. A little before half the programme had been gone through I noticed one of the Emperor's messengers enter the building. He was dressed in magnificent green silk uniform, and went straight up to Mr. Nagasaki and delivered a message, which made the latter turn pale. He spoke quietly to H.R.H. Prince Arisugawa, whose visit to Europe will be remembered by my readers. He next addressed Prince Arthur, who without any delay led out one of the princesses. All the remaining princes and princesses followed two by two, as well as the whole Court. I feared that their beloved Empress must have died, but before I had time to think a note from Lady MacDonald was placed in rny hand, saying that an awful earthquake was expected, and that I must come out quietly with my charges, telling no one, lest a panic might be caused. I spoke to the Prince, suggesting that we should get out quickly and have some refreshments, as there was a break in the entertainment. On leaving I looked back and saw Sir Claude and Lady MacDonald standing together, and both remaining behind. I could not but admire their quiet courage and unselfishness. They were, apparently, determined to see everyone safely out before leaving themselves, and were trying quietly to warn all whom they could. My note had been one of the first intimations. It was an appalling feeling to be in that huge European building, expecting that the earth would open any minute and swallow us up. The exit with the Princess and her brothers was no easy matter. Her walk was exceptionally slow, as befitting a princess of the old-fashioned school, and the relief was very great when we were actually out of the building, and I could explain matters.

A surprise awaited us outside, and a scene such as had never been witnessed before or after. Everyone had turned out of their houses, apparently all having been warned. Even the hospitals were emptied and the patients laid on the ground outside.

We managed to procure our carriages and drove home, seeing very interesting sights on the way in connection with the expected earthquake. On reaching the house, its inside appearance was quite as startling. The fires in all the rooms had been put out, and one or two buckets of water placed by the side of each fireplace. All the china ornaments had been taken off the tables and mantelpieces, and placed on the floor, and every door was wide open as a means of escape. It being wintry weather, the cold was terrible.

I had accepted an invitation to dine at the American Legation and to go to the theatre afterwards, but I wrote to excuse myself, not liking to leave the Prince and his brothers with the earthquake impending.

We sat in expectation, doing nothing, the monotony being sometimes broken by the delivery of a telephone message. One message, which came from a very dependable source, told us we should not be safe until after midnight. We all went to bed, however, keeping every door open, with watchmen guarding us. The Court itself must have received more reassuring reports, as Prince Arthur and many princes and princesses attended the theatre.

Midnight passed and the next day arrived, but no earthquake took place. It was a false alarm, a city scare. Who set the report going, and how it was that people all lost their heads so as to believe it, has never (so far as I know) been discovered. I heard various explanations as to the why and wherefore, but whether there was any truth in what I was told I cannot say. It remained a mystery, and also seemed to be a painful subject to the Japanese, who never alluded to it unless obliged. They had taken such untold pains to entertain their Royal visitor, and to do all in their power to make his visit enjoyable, that for this hitch to take place instead of all running smoothly was a very great disappointment. The theatre performance, however, was a great event to many of the princes, princesses and nobility, as it was their first experience of the delights of the stage, since the Japanese nobility never had attended theatres in Tokio before Prince Arthur's visit.

On the occasion of the former earthquake, which had taken place in the morning, the Naval School in Etajima was considerably damaged, and it was almost miraculous how the cadets escaped injury. It appears they were all out in the grounds at the time. A cadet told me that all he knew of it was to see part of the structure falling down. It is strange how one never feels an earthquake out of doors. You may return to your house and find there has been a great shock, sometimes even a dire catastrophe, while you were walking along quite unsuspecting.

CHAPTER XVIII

DURING the course of 1907 a great proof of the trust placed in me by the Prince and his guardians was shown in my being allowed to take my three youngest charges for a trip to Korea and China. On this occasion we were accompanied by only two gentlemen, my interpreter, the amah, and a man-servant. This trip seemed to me to be the crowning of my years of work in the education of these young Princes. It was hoped that to go over the battlefields where their brave soldiers had so valiantly fought and died might awaken in them a sense of their own insignificance, and the need of preparing themselves for the great possibilities of life which lay before them, and might impress on them the duty which they owed of service to their Emperor, their country, and their fellow-men. My great triumph lay in the fact of our taking no medical attendant with us.

When this intended trip became known I received a few letters of protest from various friends, some of whom had been over this ground, advising me strongly not to attempt it, for both sanitary and other reasons; but I believed it was essential for the development of the characters of these young boys, and, strong in the faith that right ever conquers, paid no attention. With a huge medical book under my arm, and a fairly large medicine chest, we started on our way.

We left Tokio on June 29th, reaching Kobe the next day, and went straight through to Shimonoseki, arriving at 8 p.m., when we went at once on board the boat Tsushima Maru 9 which was packed so full that we could only have four cabins to share between us. The boys and the two women were shocking travellers, both in the boat and the train.

We reached Fusan, our first touch with Korea, about 9.30 a.m. From the boat the hills looked sandy, hot and bare; the soil is khakicoloured, quite different from that of Japan. There were three small Japanese cruisers in port.

When we landed the first thing that caught my eyes was a long row of Korean coolies with wooden boards on their backs for carrying luggage, terribly heavy things in themselves, apart from any burden. Afterwards I saw one of these men resting on the road: he had removed the carrier from his back, which was turned towards me, and was quite bare. At first I thought he was tattooed all over, but discovered that the blue marks were bruises made by the board pressing on his skin.

They seemed quite jolly and happy, and are big in comparison with the Japanese. They are beautifully built, and their skin is a rich brown, not so yellow as the Japanese; they have very smiling faces and good teeth, and wear baggy trousers and a jacket. I was told that an ordinary Korean has but one suit to his back, which is seldom washed, for the simple reason that its owner would have to remain indoors during the process; also, for the same reason, they do not work on a wet day. The married men have a little knob of hair on the top of their heads, and the unmarried have their hair parted down the middle and plaited behind. It is very amusing to see the Koreans wearing high hats with this knob peeping through, the hats being more or less transparent, like a meat-safe. Sometimes they put little oilskin umbrellas about a foot long over the hat, to protect it either from the rain or the sun.

One of the Korean peculiarities, apparently, is to leave the stomach uncovered, but, except for that, the men are pretty well clothed. They carry their money and tobacco in bags swinging between their legs like a sporran, and when walking carry in their hands long tiny pipes, like those used by the Japanese. A working coolie may tuck his pipe and box of matches in anywhere, but they are most often seen sticking out of the cloth which is tied round his head. The Koreans wear shoes something like the Chinese, and white tabbis like the white sock of the Japanese, only the big toe is not separate. The better class have just the same make of clothes, but they are fashioned of a kind of yellow gossamer silk, their hats being fastened under the chin with a chain of jewels, not, I fancy, of great value. The money is kept in a vest under the coat. I saw one man with long cuffs on his arm, made of basket work, which, I was told, were worn to keep perspiration from the sleeves of his coat. They also wear basket-work bodices, and the most extraordinary hats, some of them as large as our washing baskets at home. A man whose parents have died must wear one of these immense hats for three years, and may not discard it even when at work: it is supposed to hide his grief from the prying eyes of outsiders. During the mourning period fish may not be eaten, or even touched, a somewhat trying custom for a fish-seller, especially in Fusan, where fish is the principal article of food.

As one travels by train, one sees mounds of earth dotted about promiscuously, which, it appears, are graves; they bear neither names nor inscriptions, for the Koreans bury their dead just where they feel inclined, even in ricefields. Both the funeral rites and the feasts are much like those of the Japanese; but the Koreans hire mourners, and the more wailing and weeping the greater the honour done to the corpse. Japanese usually send food for the burial feast to the tea-house, or place where it is held, but Koreans bring the food with them: you see it being carried in the procession, I did not discover where they eat it.

At a wedding mourners are also hired; the more crying there is, the more important is the bride. A girl is kept very much shut up by her parents till her marriage, and wears a head covering similar to a nun's, made of white butter-muslin. After the bridegroom has taken her away she may not go back to her parents for thirty days. She may then return for one day only, and after that one visit is not again allowed to go home for three years.

The women's dress is very quaint and picturesque. A full, pleated skirt of gossamer material, and cut very long behind, is worn over trousers, and above this is a little zouave coat between which and the waistband is a hiatus of peau nue. The women carry all parcels and packages on their heads, but few of them are to be seen about in the streets as they are kept very much indoors. I found it somewhat difficult to distinguish between the boys and girls their gentle, effeminate faces all appeared to me to be alike.

To go back to our doings. In Fusan we went to a semi-Japanese hotel, and as there were only four rooms to be had I took the two big ones, side by side, for myself and the boys, and let the two gentlemen have one, and the two women the other. The boys had eaten nothing, and looked very white and limp. I had just ordered food for them, when Mr. Hirata came and said that if they wanted to visit the abode of their ancestors (one of their objects in coming) we must leave at once and catch the eleven o'clock train, and asked if they were to go on or not. I felt it would give great dissatisfaction if they did not, so I thought, even if they fainted, it would be wiser to go on. Whereupon, without having anything to eat, off we went in jinrickshas. The roads to the station are appalling, and so stony that anyone at all ill could not endure the jolting. The train we got into, which had a luncheon car, proved not to be the right one, and in eleven minutes we had to change at a place called Sanroshin. Mr. Hirata asked if we had not better return, as there was no food to be had, but as I had secured some sandwiches and biscuits from the first train I said we would go on. We changed, and waited for the train, and the boys got better and ate sandwiches, and all went well. There are no first-class carriages, so we went second. The heat was terrific and the journey rather trying, but eventually we reached Baysan, where the children's ancestor had fought as a general three hundred years ago. There were only a few jinrickshas to be had, so we took what we could get, and went straight to a Japanese hotel to inquire for the spot where the ancestor fought, and where he had his castle. The hotel was opposite the sea, a lovely place, with a very refreshing breeze. We went upstairs and there was a balcony, where we sat and much enjoyed the rest and lovely view. My relief was great when I learnt that the spot where the ancestor fought was a particular mountain some miles away, and that it was quite inaccessible. So we viewed it afar off.

The Korean ponies are most fascinating, and are even smaller, I think, than Welsh ones: there was a perfectly sweet little foal which the boys greatly wished to buy. They seem, however, to be quite strong, for we saw a tiny thing ridden by a huge Korean, and both rider and beast appeared to be quite happy.

The streets were full of strolling natives; the usual thing, evidently, is to hold a pipe in one hand and a fan in the other. We stayed in the hotel until about three o'clock, when we had some Japanese food and caught a train back to Fusan, arriving there about seven o'clock, tired out. On the way we had to change trains again and wait an hour, so we went for a walk to a little village. Koreans all seem to live together in straw-thatched huts close to each other. The roofs are lined with roping, whether for beauty or to strengthen them I cannot say, probably for the latter reason, as the winds there are so strong. We went and looked into a hut. The walls were of mudstone and the windows were quite small; the floor was covered with a straw mat, and lying about it were wooden blocks used for pillows in sleeping. The hut seemed to be heated through a hole in the wall, by a fire burning outside. I was much struck by the way in which we were received, we were not stared at half so much as we should have been in an outof-the-way place in Japan. The people looked very dirty, and many of the children had no clothes: their hair is not black, like the Japanese, but has a certain amount of colour in it or would have, if the dust were only shaken out of it. The dust everywhere was really terrible.

From Fusan we went to Seoul, ten hours' journey in the train, and as we were tightly cooped up we found it very tedious, although we jumped out of the carriage and stretched ourselves whenever we had the chance. The food was hard and not at all good, but we had tea and chocolates with us, so it did not matter very much. After luncheon we tried to sleep, and a sudden storm came on and soaked some of us before we could shut the windows; but as I had a change of clothes ready for each of us we felt no ill effects from the wetting. After the storm the air was delicious, so fresh and bracing it reminded me of Canada, especially as there were herds of cattle grazing by the track almost the whole of the way.

Before the end of our journey the boys were thoroughly tired out, but they had enjoyed it all tremendously and had made friends with three American women, rather to the consternation of the gentlemen who were with us. One of them afterwards wrote to Zunoski on a card saying they were " three very nice boys dressed in khaki." Zun wrote back saying he agreed, etc. She wrote and asked if he liked her, but at this point he grew embarrassed and ended the correspondence. The jinricksha ride from the station to the hotel was slightly alarming. All the electric lights had gone out, and the streets were lit by lamps. The traffic was awful; the roads were thick with mud and there were innumerable carts drawn by bullocks. There was also a queer sort of train running on a narrow line, with a shut carriage in the middle and seats each side, all crammed with people.

On reaching the hotel the foreign part of it proved to be impossible, so we settled to go to the Japanese part. The luggage did not come for quite a long time, as the mud was too thick to hurry carts along. However, we settled down at last. The boys were bothered by mosquitoes, which were very bad, and the noise in the hotel was terrible, but I was too tired to be kept awake.

On the following morning the bath was, as usual, a source of considerable difficulty; but Hanna, knowing my weakness for water, had arranged as best she could, and I was conducted to a sort of tub which was being filled by two Koreans. They evinced the deepest curiosity in the proceedings, and would, I am sure, gladly have stayed and watched me, but at last I got rid of them, only to find that my bath had already served the same purpose before, and that the water was far from clean. It is absolutely appalling to have to use the same water as other people, but I should never have washed at all in Japanese inns if I had not schooled myself to do it.

After breakfast the Princes, Mr. Hirata and myself went to call on Marquis Ito. We had to wait for half an hour in a long foreign room, where all the windows were tightly shut. The room was not pretty, but it was very full of furniture.

The Marquis arrived in full uniform, as he was going to the Palace to take Admiral Tomioka and some other officers for an audience. He spoke almost entirely in English to the boys and was very nice, and full of compliments for my work, etc. He promised to send his private secretary to take us over the old Palace.

After that I left the boys, and they went to call on Colonel Nodzu, and later on Colonel Nodzu and two officials from Marquis Ito fetched us to go to the Palace. The heat was tremendous.

The Palace is only fifty years old, and was built by the present Emperor's father, a tyrant who taxed the people for this purpose, much against their will. During its building much of the timber was burnt out of spite, but still the Emperor persisted in the work. It stands in a beautiful situation, with hills all round, but the country-side is very bare, the trees having been cut down for building purposes. We could see that some of the hills had ridges on them, which Colonel Nodzu told us were planted with trees, so that in years to come it would not look so bare.

The building itself is thoroughly Chinese. We went through endless large gates the main gate was a pagoda of two storeys and through this we passed into an immense stone court-yard, full of weeds and very neglected. Opposite the gates were large halls used for banqueting, the roofs of which were dotted all over with little stone animals. It was a tiring business walking about in the heat, and finally I decided to rest and let the others go on alone. I sat down by a green stream, and watched a woman washing clothes. They looked yellow and brown, and she rubbed them on a green-looking dirty stone, whacking them now and again with a wooden stick bad for the clothes, but the effect was dream-like, they got pure white.

Prince Ito, or Marquis Ito, as he was in those days, was a strange and intensely interesting personality. In his early youth he had been under the influence of an almost unheard-of teacher called Yoshida, who was the sole inspirer of his young life, and who awakened in him a longing to devote himself to change his country for good, and to bring Western progress to bear upon Japan. Little his master knew, as day by day he quietly poured into his ears his own advanced political views, how great a statesman his young pupil was destined to become.

What wonderful material had this obscure Yoshida in his hands, and though, alas, he never lived to see Ito in all his greatness, he knew, perchance, that his labours were not in vain, and that they would one day bear fruit a thousand fold.

This far-seeing Yoshida endeavoured in vain to send his pupil to Europe, but later on, through the influence of some British shipping agents, young Ito and his friend, Inouye, the well-known Minister of Finance, managed together to reach England. There they studied with all their zeal, as perhaps only Japanese students, inspired by love of their country, know how to do.

Upon the return of Ito to Japan his life's battle began. Full of noble and ambitious ideas, burning to bring about great political changes, in those early days he nearly lost his life and was on one occasion hidden away in a dust-bin, as the only way of escape. His nature knew no fear, his dauntless courage and determination brought those things to pass for which his soul yearned and for which he would gladly have laid down his life. He played a conspicuous part after the overthrow of the Tokugawa Government in a social and political revolution. Four times he held the high office of Prime Minister, and it was he who, with one or two other great men, encouraged and guided the marvellous military and industrial development which has now placed his country amongst the great Powers of the world.

The present constitution under which Japan is now governed is in a great measure the work of the Marquis Ito. He was honoured with the intimate confidence of the Emperor, and was selected by his Sovereign to proceed to Europe to study the forms of constitutional government in the various Western nations.

When about to retire from public life the Emperor sent him to Korea as resident general, during the time of the Russo-Japanese war.

This must have been a great strain upon him, now well advanced in years; but he was ready to take up his work for his revered Imperial master.

When it was my privilege to visit his house I was struck by the simplicity of his surroundings and the absence of all display of wealth.

The Marquis Ito was not a worshipper of this world's goods, and when he died he left but a small fortune behind him. I can see him now, so kind and thoughtful, so gracious in manner, as he welcomed us to his home.

His appointment to Korea involved very difficult and important work, including the education of the young Crown Prince, or, rather, the new Emperor of Korea.

How piteous it is to think that the life of such a man should be ended by the hand of an assassin!

CHAPTER XIX

THE next place of call was Chemulpo, where we had certain experiences which I shall not easily forget. Leaving my party at the station I set out with Miss Nischiki to arrange rooms for us at what appeared to be the best hotel; but it proved to be under Chinese management, and was quite impossible. However, having heard that rooms were to be had at a Japanese club I made my way there, and demanded accommodation, not without misgivings, for, although better than the hotel, it was far from a desirable spot. The Japanese man and woman in the office were obviously not at all anxious to take us in, but I persevered, until eventually we were promised four rooms. I then sent Miss Nischiki to retrieve our party from the station, and stayed at the club, where I heard an amusing conversation in the smokingroom between a foreigner and a Japanese. The former said that I was Mr. Hirata's wife and that the boys were my children; and they discussed mixed marriages, both entirely disapproving of them. The party turned up soon, but in the meantime the two proprietors had quarrelled over my coming, and got disagreeable, so that finally, when my charges arrived, they refused to take us in! I heard afterwards that it was solely a man's club! I cannot describe what I felt, nor how hopeless it all seemed when I saw the loads of luggage filling up the narrow street and had nowhere to put them.

However, we heard of a Japanese hotel right in the port, so off we went. It did not turn out so badly, though the bath water was dirty and full of insects; so we could not wash. The food was really bad, but we ate biscuits and chocolate. We could get nothing to eat until nearly four o'clock. We were all tired and lay down, but not for long, as Admiral Tomioka called to ask us to dine on his flag-ship. There were three ships in port, the Hashidate, Itsukushima and Matsushima; the former was the flag-ship. At five o'clock we were fetched by an officer, and went in jinrickshas to a nice little launch, which took us to the ship, where Admiral Tomioka welcomed us. He is one of the most charming of men, and was very kind to us all. We had a delightful little dinner, and afterwards the children and I went out and left the men to smoke. It was a heavenly night, the sky was full of stars, and there was a delicious soft breeze. Upon leaving, the launch took us back to the shore, where we found only one jinricksha, which Mr. Hirata put me into, telling the man to take me home; but the two boys were so thoughtful that they ran by my side the whole way because they did not like me to go alone through the streets so late at night. The attendants do not think of these things, but now and again the Princes open their eyes. We got back about ten-thirty and went to bed. The hotel had no good futons (mattresses), and we all felt quite bruised in the morning, they were so hard; but I managed to sleep. The heat was truly awful.

The next day we sat indoors all the morning, and tried to eat Japanese luncheon at twelve o'clock in order to be ready to catch a boat for Dalny at one o'clock. When we reached the place where the launch was waiting there was a big crowd to watch the arrival of the Marquis Ito, who was to lunch with Admiral Tomioka. As we stood and watched the procession pass they saw us, and he and the Admiral walked towards us to greet us, Marquis Ito again speaking only English. After they left we went to the boat in a launch lent by some officer, who came and shook hands as we left, saying, " God be with you." Rather nice, I thought.

The journey to Dalny was not so trying as I expected it to be, and we did not have a bad night, considering that we were all in a secondclass cabin, consisting of a big room with twelve bunks. All the first were full. The sea was beautifully calm all the time, and we reached Dalny two hours before we were due. It was an awful business landing; there seemed great difficulty in getting the boat near enough to the pier. The whole scene was a great contrast to Chemulpo port, where the Koreans all wore white or buff colour; in Dalny they were all in Chinese blue.

A very noisy, excitable crowd it seemed to me. The head of the police was there, and some officers, to meet the children; it was a trying ordeal. There were about four carriages lent by officers. Zun and I went in the first one, and two mounted officers rode in front. The horses were very fresh, and driven at an awful pace. One of the riders' horses shied just by our side and the officer was thrown, but he managed to pick himself up. Since that time, after having had various near shaves in driving, I have heard a good deal more on the subject than I knew then. It appears that all the horses there are Russian and have been driven by Cossacks; the drivers who replaced them are Chinese, who drive recklessly and cannot manage some of the beasts at all. Mercifully, it was raining fast, for the dust in Dalny was indescribable.

The Hotel Kyoto, in which we stayed, was mostly Japanese, except for two small foreign rooms, one of which I took. It is about three hours by train from Dalny to Port Arthur. At the station was a Russian woman who had a cross on her dress, possibly in the employ of the Red Cross. She was very irate with the Chinese boys there, as they had, apparently, interfered with her luggage; she smacked one of these boys' faces, and greatly entertained us by her fury.

There were plenty of battlefields to be seen between Dalny and Port Arthur, miles of deep trenches made by the Japanese, and many mounds where the dead were buried. The houses were mostly roofless, the Chinese having taken off the wooden roofs and plundered right and left. There was a man in the train who volun teered to explain things to us as we went alonj; and who pointed out in the distance the famous 203-Metre Hill.

On arriving at the station the children were met by Captain Seki, who had carriages waiting for us; he was a very nice man and spoke English fluently, having been trained in our Navy at Greenwich. Zun and I drove first, and an engine, screeching in one of the horses' ears, startled the beast and it began to bolt, but the driver managed to pull it in.

I must not forget to mention that both in Dalny and in Port Arthur carriages take the place of jinrickshas, sadly tumbled-down affairs, drawn by a pair of horses which are hardly worthy the name. These dusty conveyances, with wheels often half off, are packed full of boxes, coolies, everything and anything knocking up against each other, and are all driven by Chinese boys. Oh, the awful dirt! We drove to Port Arthur Hotel, Captain Seki leaving us and promising to come again later on.

The hotel was horribly dirty. The three boys and I had small foreign rooms adjoining, at the top of a wooden flight of stairs. My bedroom door had had a shot through it and everything was terribly sordid and dingy, but my faithful amah, as usual, cleared things up, and made us as comfortable as possible. It was interesting to hear the twelve o'clock gun from Golden Hill, a well-known point during the war.

One night we dined at Admiral Hashimoto's private house. He was the head of the Admiralty, and the dinner was most interesting. He lived in what had once been a big Russian school, the furniture, stoves, etc., were all Russian. We were met at the door by the Admiral himself and all his officers, and by three little Japanese ladies, of whom one was his wife, and another, Madame Saisho, sister-in-law of Admiral Togo, a charming little woman. It was a very stiff party at first, and there was much ceremony shown in presenting the officers to the young Princes. We sat in a double sittingroom, the officers and children in one room, and I and the three ladies in another. The three boys were seated on a sofa and viewed afar off. Madame Hashimoto and the third lady were quite silent. Madame Saisho could only speak a few words of English, but Captain Seki came and interpreted for us.

At last dinner was announced, but the going in was a lengthy performance, owing to questions of precedence. The table held twenty and the dinner was foreign. There was a lovely decoration in the middle of the room, consisting of the trunk of a tree, around which azaleas and other flowers were placed at various points, as only the Japanese can do; the effect was most beautiful. Dinner was a long affair, but as the men on either side of me spoke English we had a good deal of fun, and ended the meal by drinking each other's health all round.

After dinner we went into a room where the band was playing; they played very well. The programme had been especially selected for me, and one of the admirals had ordered a selection of old English songs. We had the " Minstrel Boy," among many others, and I felt it a bit difficult to keep my eyes dry, for we had been talking so much of the war and the awful suffering it had entailed. Round us were the hills where thousands had been killed, and we could see the sea and the place where Commander Hirose had so heroically died in trying to blockade the port. What with the music of home and the stars overhead, one realized how short the distance is between life and death.

After the band ceased we went into the drawing-room, where an old Japanese man played the biwa, a stringed instrument, to which the player often sings war songs. The actual singing is ludicrous, more like wailing; but, knowing the subject of the songs, I watched the man's face, and could see how he felt his war song. Admiral Hashimoto seemed very impressed with the fact that the biwa was at last played in Port Arthur.

The next day Captain Yamashita and General Saisho's interpreter fetched us to go over the Russian fortresses, six in number. The party went over three, but I could only manage two. The driving there was alarming. Miss Nischiki and I had to cling on to each other; we were continually on the point of being thrown out. We had to drive over steps on the way, and across short deep ditches. Anything and everything seemed to be possible. On our way we passed many fine buildings; it was sad to see huge holes made by shot in these lovely houses. There is an old city and a new one not yet finished building, and there was a large foreign hotel, which was used by the Russians, but is now converted into law courts.

All the barracks were empty and had no windows left. The fortresses were high, steep hills of rough stones, wonderfully and cleverly designed, with subterranean passages. I went into one of these; the smell was dreadful, and I saw pieces of fur and many traces of Russian soldiery. The interpreter told us how in one of these passages the Japanese had met the enemy face to face, having dug a subterranean passage themselves. The first fort we went to was Pine Tree Hill, the scene of a great contest with General Nakamura in command, who arranged his forces zigzag, so that no great number of men could be aimed at by one gun. There was a little village in the valley beneath, which was inhabited formerly by Chinese, who fled during the war, but have now returned to their homes. We drove to the second fort, Dragon Hill, which we all went over; and then to the third, Wan Tai. It was very hot, so I sat down, and the interpreter told me no end of wonderful things about the war.

We reached home about six o'clock, and all got ready to dine with General Saisho, Commander-in-chief of the Japanese Army in Port Arthur. This dinner was much less ceremonious than Admiral Hashimoto's. His house is next to General Steussel's, a lovely large place with a huge balcony outside the diningroom, and lots of stone steps leading into a garden.

After dinner we went out on to the balcony, and were shown specimens of scorpions which are to be found in Wai-hai-Wai, a pleasant piece of news, as we were on our way there! They are rather like prawns or big shrimps in size, but of various colours. The usual one is black in body, but the one whose sting is fatal is white. They gave me two or three in a bottle of spirits. These scorpions get between stones and come out on fine evenings. If you are stung by a very bad one, all you can do is to cut away the flesh that may possibly save you.

The following day we were again fetched and drove off to the 203-Metre Hill, where the deadliest of all the battles took place. It was a long drive, but most enjoyable. This time Miss Nischiki and I had a safer carriage, a private one. We passed many Chinese on the way; the children were clotheless and ran after us for money. It was terribly hot, and the climb was very steep and difficult.

After this we drove to the Admiralty, where we were given luncheon. Admiralty House is the one in which Prince Alexieff lived, with a large dining-hall. The table was laid half in Japanese style and half in foreign. Admiral Hashimoto sat at one end of the table, and the admiral next in rank sat at the other. All the officers spoke English, and we were a cheerful party.

We next went with the interpreter to the museum, which I found to be one of the most interesting places in Port Arthur. There is a gun there with " Dieu et mon droit," and a crown a British gun, made by Krupp, with General Eardley-Wilmot's name on it. It was taken by the Chinese from the English during the Boxer troubles, again from the Chinese by the Russians, and afterwards from the Russians by the Japanese, who have had large offers of money for it, both from a British general and from Krupps, but who will not sell it. The museum is full of uniforms, clothes and underwear, and even a pair of ladies' white satin shoes are to be seen.

Certainly my visit to Port Arthur increased my respect for the Russians. They knew how to fight, and fought heroically, and their war preparations were marvellously clever.

Admiral Hashimoto, General Saisho and all the officers were at the station to see us start for Dalny. I felt quite sad at leaving, for everyone had been so nice. We left for Newchang, a journey of twelve hours, which proved to be rather a strain, as Hanna became ill and nearly fainted, and there was no place where we could get water. She kept telling me that she knew she would die of an illness called "gorilla." I did not understand her at the time, but discovered afterwards that she meant "cholera." This journey was the most trying of all we had experienced on the trip, but an hour before we reached Newchang, Hanna got much better. I had medicine and brandy with me in the train, and nursed her till she quite recovered.

Mrs. Kubota, the Japanese Consul's wife, whom I knew before she married, met us. The Consul also was there with some officers, and put the boys into one carriage and Mrs. Kubota and myself in another. The carriages there are the shape of broughams, only the sides and back have white shutters for air, as is usual in the East. A policeman on a bicycle escorted us to clear the road.

The next day we left for Chifoo, taking two junks to reach our boat. The Chinese quarrelled most dreadfully, and there was a fine fuss among them as they each wanted us to use their own particular junk. They were very dirty, and many of them were marked with small-pox.

The boat, Chifoo Maru, was a beautiful one, and we were fortunately able to secure firstclass cabins. Mr. and Mrs. Kubota came on the boat and remained on board till she started. We had an ideal afternoon, evening and morning, and none of us were ill. The food was excellent and the bath quite nice; in fact, everything was extremely comfortable, and at last we came within sight of Taku Fort. The gentlemen asked if I would stay two days on board whilst she anchored there, but I decided to go on to Tientsin, as there would be painting and shipping of cargo.

We left by a small tug at about three o'clock. The heat was beyond description and the tug was packed full. The descent to the tug was difficult, down a rope ladder. It is terrible taking Japanese women about on these occasions; they are so timid, and more than once I felt inclined to lose patience with my party. We reached Tongku and had a special carriage put on to a goods train, and an hour and a half later arrived in Tientsin. For some reason I felt almost home-sick on the train. The heat was awful, no one could speak Chinese, and everything was very difficult. They all wanted to go to a Japanese hotel, so I consented; it seemed safer as we could not speak Chinese, and the gentlemen kicked against a foreign one. Oh, the heat and fatigue! How I longed for an English voice and also English food, but only Japanese food could be obtained. However, we went early to bed. The heat was terrible, water running down our faces. I managed to sleep, but was awakened by Mr. Hirata cleaning his teeth a particularly noisy and painful process.

The next day we all went by jinrickshas to buy sun-helmets as the sun was dangerous. After that we returned to the hotel, rested, and then went sight-seeing, in spite of the awful heat. We went in carriages; the coachman and betto wore white helmets with a red brush on the top like a hearth-brush one has at home, and their driving seemed to beat the record for danger. We went into the heart of the city so as to see Chinese life, which I should not have allowed if I had known where we were going, as I heard there was scarlet fever there. We drove through street after street, all very narrow and dirty; the walls and houses were of mud. There were hundreds of naked children and crowds of men, but I saw only a few women.

In turning the corners we met with real difficulties. Often the space was too narrow. One little dog had its leg run over. One of the horses in my carriage kicked so much that the bettos had to hold him, and even then he nearly bolted. The quarrelling was terrific, and once or twice the Chinese police tried to stop our driving, but the drivers went on in spite of their protests.

We first stopped at an old Chinese city gate, like a double pagoda. We got out and went up two flights of stairs, all dark, very old and stuffy. At the top we had a bird's-eye view. There was a shaky old rail round and a narrow path to walk upon, which made me very giddy. After that we went into a very old Mahomedan temple, and on the way back were taken to the new station to be shown the broad streets, of which the citizens are very proud.

The next day we returned to the steamer and made for Chifoo, but were stopped on the way by a fog. When it cleared off the captain found that we were only a quarter of a mile from a dangerous rock which had sunk one of the company's ships a few years ago. We reached Chifoo and were met by the Japanese Consul in a launch.

There were no rooms to be had in the hotel, but the Japanese consul agitated so successfully that five large rooms were opened in an annexe and given to us. They had not been used for months and the dirt was a trial, but we only stayed two nights, and then went by steamer to Wai-hai-Wai, where we spent a few happy weeks.

CHAPTER XX

AS I look back from the perspective of some few years the strangeness of some of the social customs in Japan is borne in upon me. Here are a few, as they come into my mind.

A short time after my arrival there seemed to be some matter for congratulation in the house. I was told that the eldest Prince had driven off to the Palace, to thank His Imperial Majesty the Emperor. Asking what it was, Koma told me that the children's grandfather had been made a " big gentleman " by the Emperor. I, therefore, congratulated the Prince on his return, and then began to inquire where his grandfather lived. The only answer I could elicit was from Koma, who said, " He lives under a stone." I afterwards discovered that it was a posthumous honour. Streams of people came to give their congratulations; so great was this honour that it had previously only been granted to two others.

The first dinner party given in our European home had also its surprise for me. The Japanese guests all arrived half an hour before the time mentioned in the invitation. This unusual custom was a sign of politeness for which I was quite unprepared. I had not even donned my festive frock when, all of a sudden, the carriages rolled up the drive. Another surprise came the next morning, when the same carriages drove up to leave cards with messages of thanks for last night's hospitality.

The exchanging of photographs between two newly-made friends, as a polite attention, is a custom not often understood by foreigners, whose refusal unwittingly gives pain. Another quaint proof of friendship is shown in sharing a bath; so at least it was in those days. Once I remember finding my interpreter in tears, as her best friend had not asked her to share her bath.

On one occasion, when arranging the furniture in the Princes' rooms, I placed their beds, by chance, with the heads to the north, which greatly distressed the attendants, as it is only customary to do this after death.

When, during illness among the Prince and his brothers, I anxiously sought to keep the sick room quiet, and endeavoured, by nursing them myself, to ward off all intruders I discovered that politeness demanded everyone to make a personal visit to the patient. This custom presented serious difficulties with a feverish patient; to have the room thus invaded necessarily proved far from beneficial, but to stop these visits meant giving great offence. I had a similar experience myself once when ill in a Japanese hospital, as many Japanese in the kindness of their hearts came to inquire for me, and I found it an impossibility for the little Japanese nurses to refuse admittance to any of the great ladies. Rather must the patient die than show such impoliteness!

Another painful custom for one who is mourning the loss of a beloved one is that when visits of condolence are made the visitor is admitted to express his sympathy face to face. A terribly painful ordeal for both mourner and friends! On the part of the former there must be no outward form of grief. This was especially noticeable during the war. It was even expected of the relations of a father to show no grief, for to do so would be considered disloyal. The courage and endurance of wives and mothers were quite wonderful.

I remember visiting the house of a little princess, who had lost, after a few days' illness, her companion-sister, one whom she deeply loved. It was astonishing to see this young girl's fortitude. She was in full ceremonial dress, handing tea to the guests, smiling sweetly with her beautiful face of marble whiteness. The visit of condolence paid to General Nogi y when he uttered those well-remembered words of his on the death of his only son, claiming congratulations in place of condolences for having had the happiness of giving his son's life to his Emperor, is an example of the same.

Another custom that strikes one as strange on returning from such a visit of condolence is to find buckets of salt outside the entrance door of one's house, out of which you are supposed to throw some salt over yourself before entering the home, to cleanse away all defilement from contact with death. The relatives of the dead are regarded as defiled for a certain time, the period depending on the nearness of the relationship.

This added to my difficulties with the attendants. Should one of their relatives die the gentleman was isolated from the Prince and his brothers, and would sometimes give no service for several days. Latterly, however, this rule was not so strictly kept, and each year there seemed less notice taken of a relation's death. In this present workaday world, when no one has sufficient time to get through the day's work, people can hardly be forced into isolation for several days on such a pretext.

As a rule a foreigner consulted European doctors in illness, but an opportunity was made for me to visit a well-known Japanese specialist, who had studied many years in Germany and spoke that language well. His house was absolutely Japanese and we entered by the usual sliding doors, removing our shoes as is customary when the floors are covered with soft, padded matting. The spectacle which met our eyes was a strange one. Two rooms of waiting patients, all seated on the floor, showing no sign of impatience or hurry, some drinking tea and smoking, all more or less talking in a friendly way together. Fortunately for us we were not long kept waiting. Doctors during the consultation hour wear the long linen coats which are used in hospitals; they administer their treatment with little or no regard for the personal appearance of their patient, who leaves the house with patches of iodine on his throat, ointment on his face and head, or huge swabs of wool stuck in the nose, ears, or anywhere necessary for the cure.

A visit to a sale at a large silk merchant's very much resembles the inside of this doctor's house, only on a larger scale. One enters the shop to find hundreds of women seated, drinking tea. They seem to have taken root in the shop. There is no pushing or rushing, everyone waits quite calmly to get hold of a bargain. The ladies are provided with little coloured handkerchiefs (furushiki) to wrap up their purchases, instead of our commonplace paper and string.

One of the great Japanese festivals is kept on New Year's Day, when only happy subjects must be discussed. New kimonos only must be worn. No matter how unfriendly two in a household may be, disagreements must all be put aside; on this occasion you must appear happy, no matter what your feelings may be. The children looked forward to this festival and spoke of it for weeks beforehand. I soon began to realize its full importance. In the first place my amah seemed as if she were bent on a thorough spring cleaning of my room, and when I looked from my windows upon the small adjoining houses of the gentlemen attendants the soft mats were all being taken up for brushing and beating, and the wadded quilts, of general use, were spread out for the wind and sun to deal with. Everything pointed to a thorough " rout out " in the home, by way of preparation for this great festival. All dirt must vanish. There must be a fresh start made in the home. To my surprise bills began to come in, and I found these were expected to be promptly paid. As Hanna prettily put it: "Must not owe anybody money when New Year comes. Debt too bad for happy day."

Then came strange, white-looking buns of huge dimensions, made of rice, called mochi. Each occupant of the home apparently had his own allotted to him. I was given mine in my room, and found five in the school-room, of different sizes, sitting on the top of each other, the largest at the bottom. These were hailed by shouts of joy from the Princes. By and by I was urged to eat some, and it was a mystery to me where the fascination came in, one might as well eat a cold hardened bread poultice. But the children relished it, adding a particular sauce, made out of the small " soy " beans.

Outside the house were signs of joy and happiness. The posts of the entrance gates had small bamboo trees or branches tied to them, as if growing there. There was a festooning of twisted cord over the doorway, all of which, I have no doubt, had its significance; but all I could glean by way of information from Hanna was, " Everything and everybody very happy."

New Year's Day itself is truly one of the most beautiful sights in Japan. The very sun came to our aid, and I never can connect this day with dark and gloomy weather. I see it always with snow and a shining sun. The streets are living pictures, endless little girls run about in bright coloured kimonos, playing battledore and shuttlecock. Even the horses seem to wake up and jingle their merry bells. Boys shout and jump, fly kites and rush after the many street vendors of sweets and dainties. The very babies on their backs seem brimming over with fun. Oh! this sweet land of laughter and lightheartedness! It is good to start your year in such a spirit. Is not joy God's best gift?

Among the duties of this season present-giving plays a most important part, and a somewhat serious and even ruinous part, too. As a recipient one is almost overwhelmed. Shops remember their customers, and add to the harvest. The gracious little Princesses used to shower rolls of silk upon the foreign lady. It is quite expected that there shall be an interchange of remembrances between the giver and the receiver. No one must be forgotten or forget.

On the first day of the year the entrance doors of each home stand open, and never close. Streams of visitors of all and every class pass through the portals.

A large room is ready prepared, with cakes and sake, of which everyone partakes. This national wine, called sake, is made out of fermented rice, and consequently cannot be kept long, as it soon turns sour. It is taken warm and is heated by standing the little china decanter in hot water. Small china cups, without handles (such as we often use at home on our tables and mantelpieces, by way of ornament), serve as wine-glasses. The colour of the wine is pale straw, its taste is sweet and it is a strong intoxicant. On the occasion of these New Year's congratulations a visitor is expected to drink sake at each house he goes to, which is not always a pleasing or desirable custom, considering the number of necessary calls he has to pay on that day.

As a rule visits paid in Japan were of long duration, as people usually came from a distance, and as a result expected to remain to a meal or two. The carriage was put up, and the attendant servants were received as visitors in the servants' quarters. In the New Year, however, the visits of congratulation are quite short, and often consisted merely in a card being left at the door.

In our house the doors were wide open and the Prince stood ready to receive each visitor's congratulations. The house towards the end of the day felt perishingly cold, but what matter? The door must not close for the first two or three days of the New Year.

In addition to these social receptions the return calls had to be paid. The Prince and his brothers had to do their allotted share of visiting among the Court and its courtiers. The gentlemen attendants filled up all other gaps. Their duty was to see that no one was left unvisited, and they whirled about like spinning-tops in the city, shooting cards wherever they were required.

Personally, I always found it a most arduous time, as I was a unit upon whom many duties fell, and had no one whom I could appoint to relieve me. I started my New Year by jumping into a carriage as early as nine o'clock, and drove incessantly through the first day and part of the next, writing my name in the Court books and leaving cards in all possible nooks and corners. But as I sat in the carriage and looked out of the window, I got my reward. The spirit of joy seemed to breathe in the very air, and one felt tempted to exclaim " How good life is! v

The three youngest boys had their own duties to fulfil on this great occasion. One out of the three was invariably chosen by the Empress to act as page, with five others, and carry Her Majesty's train. He would start as early as 7.30 in the morning, and not return until tea time. To a Japanese the honour of carrying anything for their Empress quite forbade his feeling any regret that all these hours, which might have been spent in play, were given to this most trying and fatiguing occupation. The page's Court dress was a very picturesque one, a purple velvet suit, with knickerbockers and a short, large, loose coat, with six large white pompons three each side in place of buttons, and a white silk shirt, also white silk stockings and buckle shoes. He carried in his hand a large round hat of purple velvet, also adorned with pompons. In performing their duty these young Princes certainly used their eyes. They could give a very clear and amusing description of the various uniforms and court dresses worn by the diplomats.

Every year amongst the guests at our Christmas-tree were the various little nephews and nieces of the Prince. They were beautiful little children, with rosy cheeks and bright eyes and laughing faces. Truly Japan is the children's land. Well and carefully brought up, they are strong in body and mind.

Two of the Prince's sisters are married to Imperial princes, and when one sees their splendid looking children, it seems to promise a most propitious future for the Court.

I was much astonished one day in the garden to see a high bamboo pole stuck into the ground, from which floated a number of large paper fish, and on making inquiries learned that they represented carp, and that on the fifth day of the month of May there was a festival held for boys. In a house unblessed by a son no fish, alas! may fly, but in the case of the Prince's house we were especially favoured. Five glorious fishes floated in the wind. They looked fat and strong as the air filled their paper frames, and when my interpreter told me the significance of the carp I felt it to be indeed a happy omen. She told me that the carp of all fishes is most able to swim against the strongest currents, and is the emblem of courage and perseverance. It had therefore been wisely chosen to fly on the boys' festival, reminding them that a boy starts his fight against evil early in life, and that, just as the carp can swim against the strongest stream, so must they learn to swim against the strong currents of temptations. I could but breathe a prayer for the lives of my young charges as she told me this. Their future held promise of an influence which might prove to be a great power for good in their country.

It was considered a happy omen that the naming-day of the present Crown Prince should have fallen on the fifth day of the fifth month, the very date on which the annual day is kept.

CHAPTER XXI

ONE of the most puzzling customs to me was the adoption of sons into strange families. I was continually being introduced to men whom I knew to be brothers and who yet bore totally different names. The explanation to this was that the younger son of a family is frequently adopted into another when that family has no heir, the title being kept up by this means.

One young man, whom I knew very well, suddenly appeared with a title and name unknown to me, and only upon entering the room did I discover an old friend, whose name had to be explained.

At the end of my seven years in Japan one change in connection with marriages was noticeable in the fact of birth marrying money. The nobleman married the rich merchant's daughter. Such alliances were the outcome of much forethought, after a desire for raising the standard of her trade had been awakened in Japan. The Samurai regarded all forms of trade as beneath them, and consequently, in days gone by, the only class which engaged in commerce was one whose ideas of fairness and just dealing were far below those of a Japanese man of honour. The merchants of the past, accordingly, bore a name that commanded no respect from Western traders. But, zealous of introducing a spirit worthy of her country and of her honour, Japan now gives the younger sons of the nobility business careers and marries them into the families of merchants. It is to be regretted that the first European traders in Japan were not representatives of the highest commercial codes; indeed, their motto appears to have been:

"Do others, or they will do you."

The Japanese, who are extremely imitative, thought this "sharpness" was the correct way of doing business, but now that the Samurai class has entered the commercial world they are introducing their own ideas of honour and integrity, and will eventually exercise a controlling influence over the entire country. But even in these days, alas! the Samurai spirit does not prevail entirely.

In a letter received by a firm in London the head is described as " God-like and excessive awkward for business purpose," and it is suggested that in order to influence him the writer should " creep round same by Diplomat, and add a little serpent-like wisdom to upright manhood."

Although nearly all educated people in Japan speak English I often noticed a strange reticence in their addressing me in my own language. English is taught generally in Japan, even in the government schools every child is supposed to learn it.

This reluctance to converse in English was, I imagine, caused by a natural sensitiveness against displaying their learning, and it brought me into trouble on more than one occasion. I have known even a highly -cultured linguist, fluent in English, speak the language imperfectly for my benefit. To carry on a conversation with the aid of an interpreter hinders one's ideas from flowing naturally, and makes one appear stiff and unnatural.

In the same street in Tokio as ourselves lived Prince Arisugawa, a member of the Imperial family. His Royal Highness was quite one of the best-known Japanese princes in England, and during my residence in Japan he was sent by the Emperor as his representative on a visit to the King. He was in the Japanese Navy, and had received his naval training in England.

Prince Arisugawa had a very fine European house, and the Princess, his wife, was often to be seen driving about. She was always considered to be one of the best-dressed princesses in Tokio who had adopted European clothes. The Prince and Princess kindly gave me an audience one which I shall not easily forget! It struck me, from the beginning to the end, as quite the stiffest and coldest audience I had ever been given. It was early in the afternoon, and I was accompanied by Mr. Nagasaki, who had kindly promised to act as interpreter for the Prince.

We were ushered upstairs into a large European drawing-room, where both the Prince and Princess were seated. An awful silence reigned, which seemed strangely out of keeping with the familiar European furniture and surroundings.

After doing duty with my various bows, my august host and hostess inquired in Japanese how I liked their country and how it suited my health, etc.

This continuous interrogation got so much on my nerves that I felt I could endure it no longer. It struck me that their Royal Highnesses' remarks were very shortly worded, and that Mr. Nagasaki had added, in interpreting, several necessary additions. Having answered each question in due course I was suddenly seized with the feeling that I could continue no longer, so in an impulsive moment I said to Mr. Nagasaki:

"Oh! please say all that is right and polite for me to say." He certainly looked astonished.

At last my audience came to an end. I was given the usual dismissal.

As I left the presence of their Royal Highnesses the little villages and small farms around came into my mind. I felt that a friendly chat with an old farmer in his little cottage would have been welcome. "Kind hearts are more than coronets."

I narrate this little story to point out this strange custom of pretending to be unable to speak a foreign language, amongst even the highest in the land.

Not long after this audience I was at a large Court function where I saw Prince Arisugawa talking English fluently, and my heart sank as I remembered my interview and my fatal remark to Mr. Nagasaki.

In regard to marrying the bride is found and all the arrangements for marriage are made by ic go-betweens," who are chosen for this purpose, and who act as parents from the time the choice is made right up to the marriage, and even throughout the married life. When a nobleman's daughter is of an eligible age her name is entered in a Court book, which is consulted by the go-betweens, who choose a few names and hand them to the young man for his selection. The girl herself is not kept in ignorance, and a certain amount of freedom in the choice is permitted to both. By a careful selection and the serious consideration of character, rank, and money the choice made is often a very suitable one, and these marriages mostly prove very satisfactory.

How often the result of propinquity and the ambitious match-makers mar an English marriage! Love true love is a heavenly but not a frequent visitor; where he knocks, he knocks with angels' wings, and brings a sacred blessing with him of a most divine marriage. But for ordinary marriages much may be said in favour of the Japanese custom of a go-between.

I gathered from observation that it was not considered manly for a husband to show any signs of outward affection for his wife, nor to pay her a great deal of attention in public. In commenting once upon the happiness shown in the marriages of one or two of the couples I knew, it much surprised me to be told that the husbands were thought to be very effeminate.

There is certainly wanting in most cases that companionship between husband and wife which can make life for both so ideal. Only time can produce this in Japan, for at present girls are not considered fit to share a man's life and interest.

The great mistake of the ordinary married Japanese life is that the husband and wife are not as a rule left to themselves. The start in life together is frequently made under the roof of the husband's family, and it may even be that he marries so young that he has no independent income. A man's education lasts much longer than in England; conscription adds another two years to it, and often prevents his earning enough to support his wife. She is therefore taken into his parents' home as an additional member of the family. She has not the joy of her own little home, where she can wisely influence her husband and prove what a helpmate she can be. When the gift of children comes she is deprived of the sole care and responsibility of training them, and this is a drawback to both husband and wife.

There is a touch of child-life in this nation in their dealings with each other in this matter.

Take for example the first meeting between a man and woman. After the marriage between the two has been suggested to them it is necessary that they shall meet, so as to judge of their feelings to each other, and decide if they wish to be betrothed. It may be the meeting has been arranged among friends, in a restaurant or at a private house. The purpose is understood by each person concerned; but, to all appearances, the meeting must appear entirely accidental, and the game is kept up all through.

The amount of present giving on the occasion of a wedding must be a most serious tax on the parents, especially those of the bride. Her trousseau entails a small fortune. I was once invited to inspect the trousseau of the daughter of a well-known man. There were many chests of drawers and boxes, full of beautiful materials for dresses and sashes. The obi, or sash, having a quantity of gold in it when worn on big occasions, can be most costly. There seemed enough materials to last the bride a lifetime. The greatest surprise was in the endless household goods included in this trousseau. A beautiful writing-table with every requisite, lacquered trays for holding the Japanese meals all so complete as to include even the chopsticks, which are usually small in size for a lady's use. There are various kinds of chopsticks which may be of gold, silver, or ivory and bone. The ones most frequently in use are of wood, brought in new, and with a paper band round them such as we use for a packet of envelopes: this is proof of their never having been used before, and appears to be a most sanitary and clean idea.

In addition to these writing and eating utensils were all things for tea making and flower arrangement, and everything necessary for needlework. In fact, as I looked at the treasures, it seemed as if nothing had been forgotten, even stamps were to be seen lying in the lacquered box.

Added to these were two or three complete sets of Japanese beds. I was told that the bride would also be given endless presents by her parents, which she would distribute among her new relations, even the servants receiving an individual gift. Sometimes one meets a procession of men carrying boxes and large parcels on their shoulders. Upon inquiry I was told that this is a bride's trousseau, which is carried to the bridegroom's house a few days before the marriage. It is especially carried by men in this way, and never taken by a drawn cart or carriage. The bedding and clothes are wrapped in a cloth with the crest of the bride's father on it. The boxes bear the same crest. The longer the procession, the greater importance attaches to the bride's family. Strange to say the bride does not use her husband's crest at first. A few days after her marriage she returns alone, and visits her parents for a day or two. After this, she bids them farewell for ever as regards family ties and enters her husband's family exclusively as a member, and from that time she may use her husband's crest.

The marriage ceremony itself is unknown to me, as only near relations are ever present. Within the last few years there has been a religious ceremony in a temple designated for the purpose, in addition to the private ceremony always held in the bridegroom's house.

A Japanese woman, in almost every position, impresses one as being thrifty.

The way her old kimonos are washed and repaired is a lesson in itself. After washing them the material is spread out on boards to dry, instead of ironing them. A Japanese woman is rarely idle. Her " pets " (if I may so call them) very often taken the form of silkworms, which need great care, and are fed on mulberry leaves. When there are a sufficient number of cocoons to spin silk for making a kimono there is untold delight. These silkworms are kept in baskets, which have to be cleaned out every day, just like a bird's cage. They are an anxiety to keep for the first few weeks, as wind and damp are fatal to them.

The Japanese woman's occupations are essentially feminine, and she has a place in her home from which she is sorely missed should she at any time leave it.

The manner with which a lady draws out the book of paper handkerchiefs from her obi and selects one is very charming. These paper handkerchiefs are destroyed after use, and are far more sanitary than our own linen ones.

Japanese girls have a custom of powdering their faces and throats quite white. It gives them a ghastly appearance, as a thick, white sort of paste is used, and it seems to hide their youthfulness, which is the great attraction in our girls' appearances at home.

While still quite young in years a Japanese woman loses all her fresh beauty. As a rule she begins to shrink up and most of her hair falls out. There is generally noticeable on her face, however, a look of sweetness and patience produced by the struggles and sufferings of life. Among women of the West, it is often customary to seek to efface these marks, resorting to face massage, and using various artificial means. But is this the best way? Surely Autumn has as great a charm as Spring, and Age has a fine, spiritual beauty of its own. The strength and activity of a middle-aged Western woman are very much to be admired. How much more work she can get through than her sisters in the East, who resign themselves to old age and infirmity; and how often it is the good fortune of our older women to die in harness. It might be greatly to the advantage of both nations if their women borrowed a little wisdom from each other in these matters.

During the time of the Russo-Japanese war m y eyes were opened to the wonderful spirit of self-denial which was imbued in the Japanese nation. It gave a lesson to the world, and was the keynote of their success. Everywhere was their denial of self apparent, from prince to pauper. Verily the country might have been called " the land of do without." The Government took over no huge hotels nor buildingsthere was no necessity. Those with large houses were expected to open their doors and take in as many as they were able to. The recruits themselves put up how and where they could, no easy matter in that varying climate. We had several bouts of bitterly cold weather, but everything was accepted, and hardships, discomforts and deprivations were silently borne as a matter of course. I can remember no luxurious hospitals even for wounded officers. There were no entertainments; on the contrary, judging from the way one entertainment was received by some naval men it was clearly proved that they were all out to save their country or to die and nothing beyond that. This fact alone was uppermost in their minds and would so remain, until the day dawned.

The same spirit was shown amongst the women of Japan. There was a dead cessation of social life, everything in the way of amusement, pleasure or recreation was stopped. They set their teeth to suffer and endure until the end should bring them victory.

It was a beautiful expression of the soul of the nation.

Among old-fashioned people the putting the hand to the mouth to conceal their laughter when laughing heartily was a custom observed by way of politeness. Though the Japanese have a very keen sense of humour, yet I never found them good at taking chaff. Their feelings are too sensitive to endure a laugh against themselves as we do. In fact, I believe that we often hurt them sorely by our habit of chaffing, but they are always too polite to show it.

This same sensitiveness often makes them appear untruthful. It is understood in Japan that nothing must be said to hurt another person's feelings. To a foreigner unused to this idiosyncrasy the want of accuracy is very disappointing, but living, as I did, for many years among the Japanese, I discovered that untruthfulness is not a national characteristic, but is merely customary amongst them, and they themselves know exactly what it all means and how far it is to be taken literally.

It is intensely interesting to observe this wide difference of temperament and ideas between ourselves and our Japanese Allies. But, like ourselves, they are very sensitive, and they seem to be able to read a foreigner through and through, merely by intuition.

They are immediately influenced by personal atmosphere. If you do not like anyone, however nice and courteous you may be, you can never deceive that person. It seems impossible to hide one's real feelings from the Japanese, they are intensely penetrating. The inflection of a voice, the tell-tale faces of the ordinary Europeans, are at once interpreted by them.

And how very different are the two races! Generations of stoical endurance, of sorrow and pain, of hiding all emotions of enjoyment or happiness, have so trained this wonderful people that they possess a countenance almost incapable of expressing feeling or thought. They seldom show anger or emotion in words; but if they are deceived they never forget nor forgive. I remember meeting a European friend who had unwittingly offended a Japanese of high standing in whose employ he was engaged. No reprimand was given by his chief, no anger was expressed, no explanation was asked. He was received as usual, with the same courteous smile, but on his departure a few words of regret were expressed that there was no possibility of their meeting again. This was his conge.

The word " fuss," or the equivalent, is an unknown quantity to the Japanese. As a people they hold themselves well in hand, no nervous energy is wasted in an outward demonstration. The European might well copy their quiet way of taking things for granted, their independence and their utter indifference to death. At times their quiet, unruffled demeanour will, to the inexperienced eye, suggest a spirit of laziness. The ordinary Japanese working man does not hurry, but his work is done well and is finished up to time.

In the large offices there appears to be no pressure, no rush, excitement or strain, such as we are accustomed to in England. There is an air of quiet and even of restfulness. I was much struck with this when calling at the office of a large shipping agent in Tokio. Everyone seemed to be more or less asleep, all bustle and excitement such as one expects was lacking. But the clerks were ready for every question put to them. Various routes were minutely explained, and every kind of information was forthcoming. No trouble was too great, even to the smallest details.

This calmness is characteristic of the nation, and is due partly to temperament and partly to training. It stands Japan in good stead. The people who progress calmly and without thought of outward effect progress surely and rapidly there is no waste of force or energy, and they reach their goal more certainly than the nervous hustlers of the Western world.

It was very difficult to detect the likes and dislikes of the people of Japan, and to know what they really felt; for with them politeness is almost a religious virtue. They have such extraordinary self-control, from the youngest to the oldest, that a smile is never wanting if it avoids giving offence or hurting feelings. It made my work among them extremely difficult at times, and often gave me cause for sadness. They appeared to see and know the state of my mind and feelings fairly well, but their thoughts were hidden from me. One day I received a note from a student who was going up for a very stiff examination with these words: " Please pray your God about my examination." Considering I had never uttered God's name to him, or a word of religion, I was surprised at getting this. I also quite unexpectedly received a delightful letter from a friend of the Prince, of whom I had seen but little. On his leaving for America he wrote, thanking me for all I had done for him, and asking me not to forget him, which, needless to say, I shall never do.

This magnificent reserve is not confined to strangers and foreigners only, but even in family intercourse with each other they maintain an independent spirit of keeping their opinions to themselves. I am very tempted to think that this constitutes no mean part of the foundation upon which the nation is built, and which, together with the intense love of their country, makes Japan stand out as one of the finest nations in the world.

CHAPTER XXII

IN June, 1903, a three months' leave was given me by Prince Shimadzu, and I left for home with hopes of a presentation to Queen Alexandra. The time was very limited, as out of the three months' leave two were taken up by the journey. Alas! I had to return with my object unfulfilled, for the Queen was leaving for Ireland, and graciously expressed her regret that she could not afford me an audience. On the very day of sailing I received notice that Her Majesty would endeavour to see me, but to my great regret I was obliged to leave England on my return voyage. It was hard that my service to Japan should have lost me this coveted privilege.

Before leaving Japan, the Guardians had requested me to arrange a plan of work for the young Princes, and also to make a time-table of hours for work and recreation, with other details of hygiene and diet. The conscientious way in which Prince Shimadzu carried out every detail of this curriculum, both for himself and his brothers, was quite remarkable and was unparalleled for a boy of his years.

On my return I learnt that many small rules which I had never written down, were rigidly kept by the children. Nothing would induce the little Princes to eat jam with bread and butter. " Miss Howard does not wish it," was the dignified answer they made at a tea party with foreigners.

The Prince kept a daily diary of their doings, written in English. This was entirely his own idea, as he wished me to have a happy holiday with no anxiety about them.

Since leaving the Shimadzu family I have heard that many of the old home-rules, learned from me in their childhood, are still kept up. Truly this is a proof of great sincerity and gratitude. Prince Shimadzu, to a great extent, possessed this characteristic he is at heart a true Japanese. I fain would reveal the noble character, the unselfish devotion to his country of this Prince whom I was permitted to serve. Based upon that sincerity which alone is worthy of the highest name of friendship, his character proved strong enough to sink the prejudices of his high birth, and with all reverence, to cast aside the crusted usage of ages. Thus he stood out a man, worthy of the noblest service to his Emperor, his ancestors and his country.

In spite of the secluded life in which he had been brought up he has deemed it his duty to mix in the world, and for the benefit of his country to keep in close touch with the times. Foreign royalties and distinguished visitors to Japan always receive a hearty welcome from Prince Shimadzu and his charming wife.

A few years ago we were travelling in their country and were among their honoured guests. The scene still lingers in my heart. It was a home of youth, health, sunshine and merriment, with an additional joy from the presence of two lovely little children. The little son and heir conducted himself with the true dignity of his House showing us his toys and various treasures. After some time the strain of entertainment palled on our baby host, and smiling shyly he whispered two words to his attendant. "What does your young master say?" we asked. "That would not be polite to tell Prince Shimadzu's visitors, madam," replied the attendant. "Never mind me," I said, "I have a mother's heart." "The young master asked me," said he, "when are the foreigners going away?"

On one of Prince Shimadzu's naval cruises he went to America and paid a visit to San Francisco. A cutting from a paper sent me by an American gives the following account:

"Prince Shimadzu of Japan, also prince of good fellows, desirous of showing his appreciation of the hospitality of San Francisco, gave a dinner last night at the Tait Zinkand Cafe to prominent citizens, Consul- General Nagai, officers of the Japanese warship and other naval officers. Toasts were drunk to the Emperor of Japan, the President of the United States, and San Francisco, the golden gateway to the Pacific. The Prince made a neat little speech, expressive of the friendly feelings existing between the two countries. He hoped that those friendly relations would continue indefinitely, and doubted that the Pacific Ocean was wide enough to prevent the hands of the two nations from being joined in friendly greeting."

But my mind reverts to the early days of school entertainments, a part of my scheme of education for fitting this Prince for the wider sphere of social duties, which his position in life required of him. I recall the first time when he went with me to the British Embassy. On the occasion of a visit of one of our squadrons the British Ambassador and Lady MacDonald had issued invitations for an afternoon At Home.

The splendid reception rooms leading into each other, with their long French windows, overlooking one of the most beautiful gardens of all the Embassies, were filled with naval officers and a sprinkling of youthful midshipmen. Dancing was in full swing. The foreign community was thoroughly enjoying itself. By one of the open windows at my side stood the young Prince an expression of puzzled amazement on his face watching a form of entertainment he had never before seen.

After that, on Saturday evening we would dance amongst ourselves in the schoolroom. The Prince bought a pianola and asked a few of his school friends to join us in dancing. Our little entertainments grew in popularity, and later on we had the pleasure of receiving Prince Shimadzu's sisters and some of their school friends too.

It was not polite for me to have favourites, but two amongst the Prince's friends I held in deep affection the young sons of Prince Oyama and of Marquis Matsukata, who will never be forgotten by me. Alas! they have both crossed the borderland.

During the initiatory stage there were further surprises in store for the Prince and his young brothers. Very often I found myself an unwilling object of their curiosity, and I remember that on appearing for the first time in evening dress, I was somewhat embarrassed by the looks of sheer amazement and their simple criticism of my being so scantily attired. The consternation spread considerably when the attendants beheld me; only time could reconcile them to the vagaries of my attire.

But all this was necessary for the training of these Princes, who were too young to have seen their own older sisters thus attired. The time has now come when they are entertaining on a wide scale, extending their influence over wider worlds beyond.

I have delightful recollections of the first dinner party given at Nagata-cho, Tokio the Prince's European house. By the Guardians' wishes it was to be given on a " grown-up " scale, with due observances of etiquette after an up-to-date fashion. A short speech was therefore necessary from the young host. The principal guests were some of the Guardians, I being the only lady present. I can see him now as he made his maiden speech very white, but with perfect selfcontrol. His little brothers were bubbling over with merriment, and watching " Big Brother's " proceedings. In this old-fashioned household, hitherto, the custom had always been for the men to take precedence of the ladies. With what charming courtesy do I recall my being offered the first placeto the undisguised surprise of the young hosts themselves!

Among the many great men whom I met on various occasions are some whose names have since become familiar words in Europe.

When I think of General Nogi driving in attendance, as I have seen him, with Prince Arthur of Connaught, as far as one could see so thoroughly up to date, the news of his having committed hara-kiri (taking his own life) came as a great shock. But when I thought it over I remembered how he had behaved as President of the Peers' School. It was then he revealed himself essentially as a man of Old Japan. The methods he introduced were so spartan that it was quite an anxiety to me lest my charges should suffer through their strenuousness. On his death he left a will, in which he stated that the reason for his action was because he had lost the regimental colours in 1877. Most of the Japanese believed this to be only a minor reason, and that the real one was of a much deeper nature. They said that General Nogi saw his country gradually falling into the love of luxury and wealth and the slavery of this world's goods, and that he died to bring back to the memory of Japan the Samurai spirit, which held in abhorrence all these things and recognized only an ascetic life of self-negation. He did not die in vain, for his death made an immense impression on the people, in fact, it might be described as a setback to foreign influences.

The late Emperor was really extraordinarily simple in his life, and the room he chiefly lived in was so humble and simple that, after his death, it was suggested in one of the leading papers that it should be thrown open to the public at stated times, as an example to the people of simplicity and frugality. In a description of this room I once read that " the rugs were worn, the plastic walls blackened with soot and the paper screens were patched in many places." Surely here is a worthy memorial for his people! There was nothing suicidal in General Nogi's death. It was that of a martyr, dying for the truth of his creed. Would it not have been better if we ourselves had pulled up sooner on the downward path of luxury and selfish extravagance which has led us into the present war? My recollection of Countess Nogi was that she was exceptionally shy and retiring shall I say almost timid? But her courage did not fail her. She followed what she firmly believed to be her duty, in dying with her husband.

General Nogi also set us another example. He had lost both his sons in the Russo-Japanese war and therefore left no heir. Contrary to all Japanese customs he did not adopt a son to carry on his name, lest as he expressed it a "stranger " might tarnish the tradition which he held so dear.

I can see in my mind Prince Oyama, whose simplicity greatly impressed me, driving up to the door, with his old coachman, wearing a long beard his carriage drawn by a pair of white horses, unadorned by trappings of gold braid and buttons. His large European home was equally simple, extravagance or luxury were unknown there.

At one memorable dinner which was given at Prince Shimadzu's house, an amusing little episode took place, indicative of the calmness and self-control of this interesting personage. On this occasion there was even more than the ordinary speech- making, always an important feature in Japan at a big dinner. During the long-winded speeches, it was customary for all the company present to stand, and the guests all rose to their feet, amongst them the celebrated Field-Marshal Oyama.

The lackey who stood behind his chair in attendance upon him perceiving that a speech which had lasted for some time was about to be finished, began to push Prince Oyama' s chair towards him. At this point, however, suddenly an after-thought came to the speaker's mind, and the speech began all over again. This caused the lackey to pull back the chair. Prince Oyama, however, seemed to be unaware of the continuation of the speech, and he prepared to sit down just as the chair had been again removed. He was on my right, and all that I then saw was this great and celebrated man sitting under the table calmly waiting events, with his row of magnificent orders shining dazzlingly in the shadows.

At first I thought he was ill, for he seemed in no hurry to move, and like lightning the idea flashed through my mind that I should venture an offer to help him to his feet. Very quietly, however, a Court gentleman came to his aid and lifted him up.

The solemnity of the action and the awful stillness in the room were having their effect upon the smaller Princes. I caught sight of their faces and nodded severely at them. One of them, endeavouring to stop his nervous laughter, took a gulp of water, which, alas! he was unable to retain, and choking all over the table, he broke the silence.

The courtier began a series of bows, apologizing for the carelessness of the lackey's action; but Prince Oyama, himself a king of courtesies, returned the bow in thanking for the assistance given him by the gentleman. For a minute or two the exchange of polite bows took place. After that the dinner continued as before, and no further reference was made to the mishap.

How indicative of the true Japanese nature! That gracious consideration for the feelings of others for the host and his guests around.

The next morning, early, I drove round to ask after the Prince, lest the accident of the night before might have shaken him. I learnt from the Princess that no mention of it had been made on his return home so gracious had he been in shielding Prince Shimadzu's House from any blame due to carelessness, or casting any slur upon the dinner given in honour of himself.

It is this calm dignity and reticence, this control of self, this diplomacy, together with their intense devotion to their country, which makes Japan's great sons the leaders they are to-day. In small or in momentous events, they are ever the same; in private, as well as in public life, they are strong yet simple, adamant yet sympathetic, always imbued with one desire service to Japan and her people.

The one recollection I have of the present Crown Prince was as a very young child. He was then under the care of the late Admiral Kawamura. I remember him seated on a chair, a very small person! having a pair of European button-boots put on him, and much enjoying the treat of the new boots and the excitement of the endless buttons. He was a thoroughly natural child, full of health and fun. Suddenly he caught sight of me, and upon my making the bow which was expected of me the little Crown Prince, in the midst of his childish glee, voluntarily put up his small hand to his cap, and saluted with much dignity.

Although only a child of about three years of age one recognized the proud blood which flowed in his veins. Through my mind flashed the thought:

"You are every inch an Emperor and one day you will be a strong and powerful ruler."

I felt far more at home in Japan at their Naval entertainments than at the Military. There was such a spirit of comradeship, hilarity and goodwill amongst us all; even were I a unit among many men, which was often the case.

Wherever I went English seemed to be voluntarily spoken among naval men perfect English, too, without any foreign accent. This difference between the two services was evidently accounted for by the fact that the Japanese Navy was founded and fostered on purely English lines, whilst their Army, which was raised by conscription, was armed, clothed, drilled and organized after the best European models. In those days the system of German Militarism had not shown itself with all its brutal side so the model had been chosen in the past from Germany. The present system would be abhorrent to the nature of a Japanese.

We can see all through the Russo-Japanese war the wide difference between the Japanese code of honour and their humane treatment of prisoners and the vile brutality of the Germans of to-day. But on the surface German influence was very noticeable among the Japanese military officers. At some of their military dinners I would often feel " out of it," their entertainments appeared to me so much stiffer and colder than those of the Navy, and English was much less spoken.

It was of great interest to me that Prince Shimadzu and his brothers were very antagonistic to anything or anyone German the Prince declaring that the Germans were like ants, invading the country and consuming everything as they went. I think it was due to this remark that my eyes were first opened to the truth of the simile. Now, after nearly five journeys round the world, I am convinced how very far-reaching the simile is. They swarm everywhere and their consuming powers are not only visible, but, alas 1 audible in hotels, where I have seen them seated at their meals for hours, their appetites appearing to be inexhaustible. People say that the Germans make bad colonists and are not capable of making a little home wherever they settle, as we are. I must make reservations. They become much more one with the people amongst whom they settle than we do, quickly acquiring their language (however difficult a dialect it may be), and studying the creeds, superstitions and habits of their neighbours with all the Teuton thoroughness.

Yet when this is accomplished these travellers from the Fatherland only acquire a veneer of foreign civilization it is a case of once a German always a German. It is very rarely indeed (and perhaps only brought about by intermarriage with foreigners) that his naturalization in other countries is more than skin deep. Love of the Fatherland is imbued in the German baby from the cradle upwards.

In visiting various creches when in Germany I have seen little infants, lying in their cradle, placed with hand to head as a salute for the Fatherland by the nurses; and the tiny toddlers soon acquired the goose-step salute as they played at marching, with their tottering footsteps.

It is because of the innate love of Fatherland in the German that I view with concern in these war times a certain laxity in dealing with the naturalized Teutons at home and elsewhere. One cannot be sufficiently on one's guard. Teuton psychology makes it impossible to imagine him going against his country under any conditions.

On January 15th, 1908, Marquis Matsukata honoured me with an official visit, informing me that H.I.M. the Emperor of Japan had graciously acknowledged my work.

I was deeply gratified by so great a condescension. During my seven years' work H.I.M. the Empress had always taken a lively interest in the progress made by the Prince and his brothers.

Since my first presentation to Her Majesty many years had elapsed, and when the Royal command came for me to go to Numadzu for a farewell audience of the Empress I felt it was the crowning proof of Her Majesty's appreciation of my work.

Mr. Nagasaki most kindly escorted me to Numadzu a journey of about five hours from Tokio. On arrival we were received by Count Kagawa, the Empress's chamberlain, who, by his gracious and kindly courtesy, always won the admiration of all foreign visitors. I found a little room had been fitted up for me, and indeed nothing had been forgotten even to the detail of a toothbrush.

After a rest Count Kagawa informed me that the Empress had bestowed a great favour upon me in commanding me to come to Numadzu, as Her Majesty was there for a complete rest on account of her broken health. Only those in close proximity to the Court could realize the strain of the Empress's work during the two years' war. Her Majesty was constantly working for the welfare of the people, visiting hospitals, attending public functions, and with her own hands ministering to the care of the wounded.

The simple, unofficial home life of our King and Queen, who, unattended, will often informally receive and entertain a favoured guest, is a custom totally unknown in Japan. This innovation in freedom of access to her people on the part of the Japanese Empress, was not accomplished without a very great strain to Her Majesty. I was greatly shocked to see the change that so few years had wrought, and when the news came of the death of this great Empress and truly noble lady it was scarcely a surprise.

At the time of this great national loss we were visiting the country, and the intense love and veneration in which the Empress was held by her people was almost overwhelming. Everyone in the land goes into mourning for a whole year upon the death of the Sovereign, during which time the most rigorous rules are observed, and no entertainments of any kind are held.

On the occasion of the official visit paid by Marquis Matsukata he handed me a most gratifying testimonial, which, translated into English, I venture to place at the end of my book of reminiscences.

Translation.

To Miss Ethel Howard.

Though in order to come to our country, you had to part with your relatives and friends and to cross over the great ocean which lies between us, yet your brave spirit brought you here to Japan, where the climate and customs are quite different, and you took upon yourself the duty of the home education and upbringing of Prince Tadashige and his young brothers, in accordance with your agreement with the House of Shimadzu.

Owing to the difference in our respective modes of life, the arrangements of the household and tuition at first presented great difficulties, but the single-hearted, earnest and patient way in which you so assiduously and attentively applied yourself not only to the studies, but also to the care of the health of the Prince and his brothers, crowned your efforts with success, and the mental as well as physical development of the Prince and his brothers made rapid progress.

At the final examination of the Naval Academy, which the Prince passed last year, he graduated with success, not falling behind other cadets. His young brothers also are making steady progress both mentally and physically. This good result must be ascribed not only to your wide knowledge and great experience, but also to your earnest and unselfish devotion to the education of the Prince and his brothers.

In view of this I beg to express my warmest thanks for all that you have done.

(Signed) MASAYOSHI MATSUGATA. Tokio, January 15th, 1908.

THE END

www.ingramcontent.com/pod-product-compliance
Lightning Source LLC
Chambersburg PA
CBHW070355290526
45790CB00004B/1503